ALONE— NOT LONELY

Independent Living for Women Over Fifty

JANE SESKIN

An AARP Book

published by

American Association of Retired Persons, Washington, D.C.

Scott, Foresman and Company, Lifelong Learning Division, Glenview, Illinois

The quiz on pages 86-87 is reprinted with permission from *Journal of Psychosomatic Research*, Vol. II, T. H. Holmes and R. H. Rahe, "Social Readjustment Rating Scale (SRRS)." Copyright © 1967, Pergamon Press, Ltd.

Library of Congress Cataloging in Publication Data

Seskin, Jane.
    Alone—not lonely.

    "An AARP book"
    Bibliography: p.
    Includes index.
    1. Single women—United States. 2. Middle aged women—United States. 3. Aged women—United States.
I. Title.
HQ800.2.S47 1984   305.4'890652   84-24165
ISBN 0-673-24814-3

12345678-KPF-91908988878685

AARP Books is an educational and public service project of the American Association of Retired Persons, which, with a membership of more than 17 million, is the largest association of middle-aged and older persons in the world today. Founded in 1958, AARP provides older Americans with a wide range of membership programs and services, including legislative representation at both federal and state levels. For further information about additional association activities, write to AARP, 1909 K Street, NW, Washington, DC 20049.

Books by Jane Seskin

Living Single
Getting My Head Straight
Young Widow
Fantasy Island I
Fantasy Island II
Breaking Up
A Time to Love
More Than Mere Survival:
Conversations with Women Over 65
Older Women/Younger Men
(with Bette Ziegler)

Dedication

For Annette and Samuel Rosenblum,
Who demonstrate on a daily basis
That retirement
Is a beginning,
Not an end.

Contents

Acknowledgments

This book is a collaboration of shared hearts and minds. I gratefully acknowledge the hundreds of women who allowed me into their lives and patiently answered my questions. Their thoughts and feelings are some of the keys to our collective future.

I am grateful for the professional insights of Dr. George Getzel; Dr. Paul Nacht; Dr. Ronald Werter; Dr. Lyle Rosnick; Dr. Don Wigal; Dr. Ruth Weichsel; Harold N. Davidson, CPA; Stuart M. Rosenblum, Esq.; Paula Bromberg, vice-president of Thomson McKinnon Securities; Irving Kissin, Adelino R. Franquinha, and Steven R. Lapidus, lawyers with the real estate law firm of Abrams, Learner, Kisseloff, Kissin and Lapidus; travel agents Sylvia Levin and Sara Arthur; Claire Turett, RDH; Lee Weinberg; Ken Dawson; Frank Gonzalez; Don Domonkos; Gloria Lamm; Barbara J. Collins, JD; and Elinor Zudeck. Their input made my learning easier and more enjoyable.

Special thanks to Karina Kaulfuss, who started it all, and Marjorie L. Miller, an enthusiastic typist who always made the deadlines. Warmest appreciation to my editor, Elaine Goldberg, who provided a supportive voice and creative freedom.

And to those who never failed in their encouragement and enthusiasm for this project and for me, I'm grateful to be able to call you "friends." Thanks to Linda Breslau, Amy Chase, Gladys Dobelle, Ellen Doherty, Carolyn Goudsmit, Ronnie Greenberg, Mary Alice Kellogg, Lee Levin, Patricia Light, Mary Manilla, Beth Murfee, Chris Nolin, Susan Schatz, Ellen Schmalholz, Jane and Bob Sinnenberg, Joan Solomon, Marilyn Tessler, and Joan Weingarten.

Preface

I'm a single woman, a widow. I'm also a writer, teacher, graduate student (once again), daughter, sister, niece, friend, lover, consistent volunteer, and passionate believer in the potential of women. I believe women have choices and can make changes. I believe they are strong, nurturing, bright, creative, sensitive, resilient individuals.

My beliefs are based on experience. Since 1975 I have listened to women talk about their triumphs and tragedies. I have heard stories that have made me weep, shudder from fear, and rejoice—rejoice because a woman may be knocked down one, two, or more times, yet her spirit will not allow her to remain defeated. Through emotional, physical, or economic adversity, I've seen women incorporate and use their pain to stand taller, reach higher, and move on. I've seen them resort to laughter to deal with ugly truths, and silence to cover the wounds that continue to hurt. But I've also seen them reach out for help, get it, put it to work, and grow stronger in the process. I've seen women make difficult creative choices and decisions in terms of housing, jobs, and friendships.

I've seen them take their aloneness and rebuild and renew their bodies and souls. I've watched them sit with anxiety, sit with anger, sit with doubt. And when they could no longer sit, I've seen them take those feelings and mobilize themselves, changing the way they dealt with the world. I've listened as women set goals and watched them baby-step their way toward realization. There has been stumbling and surefootedness. But they have been out there. They have tried with halts and spurts—rethinking, reformulating, and revising their plans and purposes.

I've observed too many women recovering from catastrophic illnesses, unhappy marriages, and disappointments in life to be anything but hopeful. I've heard it; I've seen it; I've lived it. Single women can regain the control that has slipped away during moments of crisis, minutes of fear, and hours of loneliness. They can climb out of the quicksand, seize responsibility, and make a difference.

Selling cosmetics, a political candidate, or themselves, there has been a constancy of effort. And when the feet could move no longer, the voice continued, the heart beat strong, and the will pushed on.

We have caught what life has thrown at us. And we have molded and tailored each experience to wear as clingingly as scent.

1

New Beginnings

Let every dawn of morning be to you as the beginning of life and every setting sun be to you as its close; then let every one of these short lives leave its sure record of some kindly thing done for others, some goodly strength or knowledge gained for yourself.

—John Ruskin

Life. You can lie down and have it roll over you, or you can venture out, taking small steps into new beginnings.

As you age, you can choose to use the emotional and physical wear on body and soul as impetus for change—and growth.

Single, independent, there's often a freedom of spirit released by the years.

Determined, self-willed, the challenge is to become, in the second half of life, the best you can be. The raw material, like a mound of potter's clay, is there to be shaped, built up, or modified. By taking care of your present, you gain control over your future.

And those years, which many decry, are often just what's so terribly unique. Older women can draw on their wealth of life experiences and their participation in all aspects of society. The years are bench marks, signposts, merit badges. They prove that life goes on despite the tragedies, inconsistencies, and trials of daily existence. The years testify to the perseverance of the human spirit.

1

Status of Older Women

This is no story. This is our future. Statistics are there.

- □ The over-fifty group is growing twice as fast as the U.S. population as a whole.
- □ The over-fifty group has $500 billion worth of spending power.
- □ People sixty-five or over will double in number to 51 million by 2020.
- □ Those eighty-five and older—the fastest-growing group—will make up 5 percent of the U.S. population by 2050.
- □ About 15 million American women are over the age of sixty-five.
- □ Some 3.5 million American women are over eighty.
- □ Women sixty-five and older make up 60 percent of America's elderly population.
- □ There are six widows for every widower.
- □ The average age of widowhood is fifty-six.
- □ More than half of all women over sixty-five are widows, and 70 percent of those over seventy-five are widows.
- □ Six out of ten widows live alone.
- □ There are 857,000 divorced women between the ages of fifty-five and sixty-four. They make up 7.3 percent of the population.
- □ Some 467,000 women, or 5.2 percent of the population, between the ages of sixty-five and seventy-four are divorced.
- □ There are 158,000 divorced women over the age of seventy-five. They comprise 2.6 percent of the population.
- □ White women have a life expectancy of 78.5 years (compared to 71.1 years for men).
- □ Black women have a life expectancy of 73 years (compared to 64.4 years for men).
- □ One-third of older women depend on Social Security payments for 90 percent or more of their income.

Losses

No one has said that aging is easy. It's not. Physical changes might include a loss of hair; a decrease in height; a diminishment of taste and smell; atrophy of blood and nerve cells; a tendency to become far-sighted; an increase in circulatory problems; a gradual loss of memory for recent events; hearing impairment, especially for the higher tones; and greater sensitivity to cold, heat, and pain.

No one ages in the same way or at the same rate. Genes play a part in this. So does the way you live your life.

How you age, how you handle your older years, is up to you. There may be bouts of depression resulting from real losses and/or changes in health, physical appearance, employment, friends, and housing. There may be periods of loneliness, of isolation. And these may be valid feelings and appropriate actions—for a time. It may be necessary to back off for a while—to sit with the loss and concomitant change, to nurse a bruised ego and soothe a weeping soul.

One of the biggest and most wrenching dislocations for older women is the loss of a spouse, through death or divorce.

Most of us grew up with conventional scripts. The lines said to find a man, fall in love, get married, and live happily ever after. The play was supposed to end with a standing ovation, not with a woman in black bending over a casket. "Remember the Robert Browning quote," asked Lee, sixty, a widow of six months, "the one that goes, 'Grow old along with me! The best is yet to be, The last of life, for which the first was made'?" She took a deep breath and continued, "Well, that's what I expected for me and Milt. I didn't expect that I'd live the last part of my life alone."

There was another scenario. The stage directions didn't say that the glow would fade, the children would go off on their own, and so would your husband. The script didn't include a description of feelings that would make your mother blush. ("When Bill walked out, I wanted to kill! I wanted revenge so badly I thought of hiring a hit man. God, I could die when I think of the force of my anger, resentment, and jealousy. I never knew I was so possessive or that my life was so dependent on his." Barbara, fifty-eight.)

These are some of the feelings associated with widowhood.

- ☐ Anger. "How could he do this to me?"
- ☐ Disappointment. "We'd made so many plans. We were going to grow old together."
- ☐ Guilt. "If only I'd been with him, if only we hadn't quarreled, if only I hadn't asked him to meet me downtown—well, perhaps he wouldn't have died."
- ☐ Fear. "If I love someone again, he'll also die."
- ☐ Shame. "There was so much pain. I wanted it over. I couldn't stand the endless waiting, the daily hospital visits. How can I tell that to anyone? How can I say I'm glad he finally died?"
- ☐ Resentment. "How dare he die on me when we were just going to retire! After all the years of hard work and scrimping and saving, we finally had enough money and enough time to start living."

And these are some of the feelings connected to a divorce.

- ☐ Anger. "He ruined my life!"
- ☐ Disappointment. "He didn't follow the script that said 'Till death do us part.'" "I never dreamed I would be the one who walked out."
- ☐ Guilt. "If only I'd (1) lost weight; (2) got a job, left my job; (3) read more; (4) was more sexually aggressive. If only I'd been more interesting, more exciting, more attractive."
- ☐ Fear. "I'm scared to be alone. I can't take care of myself. I'll never be happy again. I'm unlovable. I'll die alone."

□ Shame. "Somehow *I* failed. I couldn't do anything to hold it together. How can I face my family and friends?"

□ Resentment. "I devoted my life to *him*. I gave up my goals and my plans to help him make something of himself. How could he reject me?"

Through death or divorce, it hurts to lose. It hurts to go from being a couple to being single. Loss is sad, often unbelievable. It shakes up the very center of who you were, who you are, and who you will become.

The divorcée's loss is intended, deliberate. There has been a give-and-take, some discussion, an agreement, some input, and a sense of control. The widow, on the other hand, has no control of events.

The divorcée may have more difficulty letting go of her anger and pain as her ex is still present, perhaps even living in the same community. Death, in fact, may be preferable to desertion or divorce, for then she wouldn't have to feel culpable.

Death may be quick. And when it comes, there are rites and rituals to follow, conventions to be observed. Divorce is not so easily marked or defined. The process may be dragged out. There may be no clear-cut rules on ending. And the pain, therefore, while similar in its feeling state of abandonment, may also be different.

We become heroic when facing the end of a marriage. Sure, you're allowed, and even expected, to cry—but then you're supposed to get up and go on. The fact is that when you are in a relationship that ends, your life is altered. You *must* start over. You must rethink and replan your priorities. Thank goodness life isn't written in cement. Otherwise, it would be unbearable.

Newly single, you may want to crawl into your kitchen or bathroom and never again come out. The feeling is understandable, but the facts are you're alive and alone and the clock is ticking off time too precious to waste. Talk out your feelings with a good friend or a competent therapist. If you're not ready for a face-to-face, write. Keep a journal. Spill your feelings onto the paper. Or talk into a tape recorder and let them go. The important thing is to release your emotions. Only then will you begin to heal.

It's necessary to mourn the end of relationships. It's necessary to work through the feelings of loss, explore the change in our status, and pledge to reclaim our lives before we can move forward. The poet Carl Sandburg said, "Life is like an onion; you peel it off one layer at a time, and sometimes you weep." It is necessary to weep when we close the door on the marriage that failed, the husband who died, the affair that ended, the child now grown, and the parent in a nursing home. And when we close the door to one period in our life and wipe away the tears, we become ready to open a door to another.

Pain

Unfortunately, pain has no time limit. Oh, how I wish it did! Then if someone asked, "How long will this last? How long will I feel this way?" I could quickly thumb through the table of pain and answer, "Ah, divorced after twenty-two years. That's approximately eight months to recovery." Or you say your heart is breaking because you put your father in a nursing home? Let me see. Under Fathers, here's Nursing home. Recovery from pain of separation is three months, two weeks, and a day. Oh, if it were so! But it's not. The only comfort I can offer is that the pain is not forever. *It will pass.* It will diminish in intensity. You will use it to grow stronger, to become more aware, to look into yourself, to pull out the reserves (skills, talent, hope, grit, and guts) you never knew you had.

Every single woman I've met over the years has *some* problem in her life. No one is immune. No one has it "all together" every moment in time. And if someone tells you she does, it's fantasy rather than fact. I sometimes think problems, or roadblocks, are put there for a purpose—so that we get to rise to the occasion, to show what we're made of, to test ourselves. (If you've been "tested" quite a lot lately, I can understand if you are skeptical.) In the words of Gustave Flaubert, the French author, "The most glorious days of your life are not the so-called days of success, but rather those days when out of dejection and despair you feel rise in you a challenge to life, and the promise of future accomplishments."

Redefining Yourself

What you take out of a divorce or a death is your self. You are a newly defined woman who has experienced pain, discomfort, despair, confusion, and a sense of unreality. Over time, if you work at it, you'll achieve a level of confidence and a freedom from the past. Over time, you'll redefine yourself. You will be a survivor!

Always single, you may have a head start on taking care of yourself. After all, you've been doing it for years. What you share with these other women is your aging, periodic attacks of loneliness, a rainbow of emotions about your past, and fleeting fears of the future. You are not alone in your concerns.

Options

This book is about you and me and the ways we choose to live our lives. There's nothing we can do about our numerical age. But we can acknowledge the choices that will help us use our years more creatively, constructively, productively, and joyfully. Some of the choices may not be pleasant. Some may be difficult; some may involve taking risks. But all of them provide an opportunity for decision making. And when we've done that, made an informed decision, we begin to take charge of our lives.

You can peer out from behind your window shades—fearful of street crime, scared of being out on your own. Or you can organize a neighborhood watch group.

You can baby-sit the television. Or you can take a course where you'll learn something that will provide you with more than an evening's entertainment.

You can quietly suffer with your aches and pains. You can loudly complain to friends. Or you can go for professional help and get relief.

You can feel guilty about depending on others for transportation. You can limit your own mobility. Or you can offer to pay, swap services, or learn to drive.

You can hide in your house, behind those old vows and memories. Or you can push yourself past the hurt and anger of being alone and begin to make a new set of friends.

You can worry yourself into the ground about your lack of money and the rate of inflation. Or you can investigate what you can offer, based on who you are, to increase your financial reserve.

You can say you have nothing to wear—nothing that fits, nothing that looks good. Or you can learn to sew, exchange clothes with friends, or haunt the thrift shops.

You can accept the way things are—on your street or in your neighborhood, town, city, and country. Or you can advocate for change.

You can continue to do things the way you did them twenty years ago because it's comfortable and easy. Or you can ride out the anxiety that often comes with choice and take a jump in a new direction.

You can cry and carry on and feel sorry for yourself that you're single. And maybe this wasn't what you had in mind for your later years. Or you can say, "This is the way it is," and make the most of your life.

Being alone as you grow older doesn't have to mean being isolated, scared, poor, sick, sad, or stuck in old habits, attitudes, or feelings. Being alone doesn't have to mean being lonely.

====================

Clara Hale, a longtime resident of Harlem, has watched over and cared for more than five hundred little children during the last seventeen years. At sixty-two, after years of cleaning other people's houses and taking care of other people's children, she decided she'd had enough. In addition to her work, this widow also personally raised forty foster children and her own three.

Whether it was an accident or providence, the now seventy-nine-year-old "Mother Hale" still had more to do. Her daughter, Dr. Lorraine Hale, on leaving her mother after a visit in 1969, noticed a woman sitting on the curb nodding off. The woman held a baby in her arms. Dr. Hale urged her to let her mother take care of the child until she was well enough to do so herself. The next day the drug-addicted young woman and the baby appeared at Mrs. Hale's door. When Mrs. Hale returned from calling her daughter, the woman was gone, but the baby remained. Word spread through the neighborhood and soon she was voluntarily in charge of twenty-two addicted children. Cribs filled the small five-room apartment.

And so the woman who'd "had enough" was then just beginning what has become Hale House, a five-story renovated brownstone in Harlem that houses a social service program run by Mrs. Hale, her daughter, and a staff of fifteen. The children, approximately fifteen at a time, range in age from one month to four years. They are left by their addicted mothers when the mothers enter drug and alcohol withdrawal programs. Hale House aims to return the children to their natural mothers, and that is usually carried out in less than two years.

"That gives the mother time to get off drugs in a program. If she's ready and the social worker checks it out, she gets the baby back. Otherwise, after three years, if the mother's not okay and the doctor agrees, the baby's put up for adoption.

"Hale House keeps me busy, keeps me working. I don't have time to feel lonely. It's just a great life, and I'm enjoying it. I love it. I'm doing the things I like. I like children. I like taking care of them.

"I think that when you're born, you've got a gift. Some people don't find it. That's why they're unhappy. But I knew from a child that I had a gift in handling children, that I could take care of children. So many of them have been happy. I didn't have one truancy in the whole bunch. And I never had an accident. The forty that I reared and the five hundred that have gone through Hale House, never one little accident. And they're happy too; you can hear it. So I think this is my gift.

"I think women should find something that they like and keep doing it. The only thing you can be happy with is what you like to do and doing it. If I live long enough, I've *got* to grow older, so why worry about it? The only thing is that when I was younger, I did what I wanted to do. I got married when I was young. And then when I got married, I had my children to support and take care of. So I have no regrets. It was a good life. It was a hard life. But I think we are born to hard things. Life wasn't meant to be easy; then it becomes monotonous, and you don't want to do things. So you just work hard and keep up. And more especially, when you see your children grow up and they turn out well—to be good, clean citizens—what else could you ask? My daughter is director of Hale House, so she takes care of all the money. I don't have to worry about that. I have a son who has his own business. He's a college graduate. And I have another son who's with the Board of Ed, a teacher.

"I don't think a person should retire. What are you going to do when you retire? Lay down and sleep? Or sleep a little later? You can get a job where your hours are less. You don't know how long you're going to be here, so why do you need to sit around and worry? You were put here to work.

"There's always been discrimination against women. That's okay. Women do what they want to anyway. They run the world really. They say it's a man's world. But it's a woman's world. We run it. And I believe that. She marries a man. He does what she asks him to do. He leaves his mother's home, and his mother has always told him what to do. He gets married and has a wife, and she tells him what to do. Otherwise he goes downhill. So women don't have to worry. They still run the world.

"I would have it so there wasn't the discrimination that there is against black people. Many other black women aren't as strong as I am, and they feel it. It doesn't bother me. It goes in one ear and out the other. I'm used to it. I've seen it all my life. So the only thing that women wish for, or that I wish for, is that my children don't suffer because being black has nothing to do with what we are inside. And God made us all like He made the flowers—different colors, different sizes, different shapes.

"I don't believe in apologizing. I don't say anything where I have to say I'm sorry. Because 'sorry' is just one of the words that comes to you after. If you've gone through everything and you've said everything and you say, 'I'm sorry,' does that take it away from you? You still remember, don't you? I tell the children, 'Sorry doesn't take it away. You've said it and you've done it, so be careful before you do it so you don't have to say you're sorry.'

"The best part about getting older is the respect you get in the street. People are so nice. When I cross the street, men run to grab ahold of my arm. And I say, 'Okay.' Then I go real slow to make them feel good in helping this old lady across the street. And when you get on the bus, people get up and give you a seat. And I had a driver and he came up—I'd been out on the street, and it was raining and there was a big puddle of water—and he ran up almost onto the sidewalk so I could step up and get into his bus. I've felt the pressure about how you were pushed around. Now they don't care about gray, black, or what. I'm an old lady—and I'm first. So this is what I like about getting older.

"I'm careful of what I eat, and I don't overeat. When I know I've had a heavy meal, I watch it. They told me I had a heart attack about seven years ago. I'll never believe the doctor, but he said I did. Anyway, I was in the hospital for seven days. It was the first time I'd ever been sick. And they had this machine there, and everybody enjoyed it. They were running around to look at it. And I said, 'Let them enjoy it. It gives them something to look at.' They came every day. They said, 'Mother, you don't know how sick you are.' I said, 'I don't. Am I sick? I may be tired, but I certainly don't feel sick. And why are you crying? I always heard people in the hospital cheer people up. What are you crying for?'

"I still go to my doctor. And he gives me medicine for my heart. I took it for as long as I thought I could. Now I go only once every two or three months. And he says, 'Oh, you're fine. You're doing just great! Continue on with the same medicine and you'll be all right.' I haven't taken any for six months. And he doesn't know. It's in God's hands. If He wants me to live, I'll live. And I pray to God always, 'Don't let me be sick lying down. When You come for me, just take me and let me go. Let me go to sleep and don't wake up.' I don't want anybody to wait on me or anything like that. So my health is good. I've never been sick, except for that one time when they said it was a heart attack. And I still don't believe it.

"I love my church, and I have an awful lot of faith. God sends me everything I want; I don't have to want for anything. When my kids were small and I was working two jobs, it wasn't too bad. It was hard work, but I'm used to hard work. My mother died when I was thirteen, so I practically raised myself. And I could've been a bum. I could have been anything."

For More Information

Publications

On Being Alone. AARP, Widowed Persons Service, Box
   199, Long Beach, CA 90801

Organizations

THEOS (They Help Each Other Spiritually)
11609 Frankstown Road
Pittsburgh, PA 15235

Widow to Widow Program
Department of Psychiatry
Harvard University Medical Center
Cambridge, MA 02138

Widowed Service Line
Boston, MA
617-371-0436

Women's Activities
AARP
1909 K Street, NW
Washington, DC 20049

Widowed Persons Service
AARP
1909 K Street, NW
Washington, DC 20049

American Association of University Women (AAUW)
2401 Virginia Avenue, NW
Washington, DC 20037
(This is the national branch. You can write for information
regarding their program for widowed persons.)

Coalition of the Concerned for Older Americans (COCOA)
105 East 22nd Street, Suite 710
New York, NY 10010

Older Women's League (OWL)
1325 G Street, NW
Lower Level
Washington, DC 20005

Gray Panthers
3700 Chestnut Street
Philadelphia, PA 19104

Books

On Widowhood

Caine, Lynn. *Widow.* New York: William Morrow and Co., 1974.

Fisher, Ida, and Byron Lane. *The Widow's Guide to Life.* Englewood Cliffs, N.J.: Prentice-Hall, 1981.

Loewinsohn, Ruth Jean. *Survival Handbook for Widows.* Washington, D.C.: AARP; Glenview, Ill.: Scott, Foresman & Co., 1984. (An AARP Book)

Lopata, Helena. *Women as Widows: Support Systems.* New York: Elsevier, 1979.

Mooney, Elizabeth. *Alone: Surviving as a Widow.* New York: Putman Publishing Group, 1981.

Seskin, Jane. *A Time to Love.* New York: Prentice-Hall, 1978.

On Divorce

Baker, Nancy C. *New Lives for Former Wives.* New York: Doubleday & Co., 1980.

Napolitane, Catherine, and Victoria Pellegrino. *Living and Loving After Divorce.* New York: Rawson, Wade Pubs., 1977.

2

The Single State

You cannot be given a life by someone else. Of all the people you will know in a lifetime, you are the only one you will never leave or lose. To the question of your life, you are the only answer. To the problems of your life, you are the only solution.

—Anonymous

You don't have to apologize for being single. It's not a liability. As the statistics demonstrate, we're growing into a sizable segment of the population. Businesses are being forced to take us into consideration. From soup for one to special weekends specifically organized for single people, we're a burgeoning market that is beginning to be written about, analyzed, planned for, and catered to.

When I think of all the synonyms for *single—solo, solitary, one, unmarried, separate, individual*—I like the word *unique* the most. To me it connotes what single women are all about. Each is special. Each has a story, a history, a public and a private self. The women who have shared their lives with me revealed a willingness to learn and a desire to use themselves, to follow new paths and to make their part of the world different from the way they found it. Sure, they continue to wrestle with problems, suffer with insecurity, and walk with doubt. But they, like you and me, continue to play with whatever cards life deals out. And many of us are choosing to use our aloneness for enrichment instead of decline.

Taking Charge

Being alone, you can't hide from decisions or responsibility. You must take charge. You must plan, revise, and carry through to action the goals of your life.

There are options and alternatives to pursue—often a dizzying array. To cut through the confusion of choices, there are professionals, various groups, and books readily available to help you cope. You don't have to be alone in plotting your life. You don't have to be alone carrying it out. You don't have to be alone being single.

As a single woman, you have the daily chance to reclaim the person you once were or hoped to be. You can revive old interests and develop new passions. You have the opportunity to test yourself. You realize you're okay without another person. You can grow at your own rate. And you have time, space, privacy, and freedom.

Loneliness

Loneliness touches every individual at some time in his or her life. It is often experienced when you feel unconnected to others. ("At holiday time, I hit rock bottom. The loneliness is unbearable. It's only recently that I've learned to take care of myself. I acknowledge the feelings but don't allow myself to dwell on them or be pulled down. I've worked too hard to get my life in order to be derailed." Glenda, seventy.)

How Other Women Handle Their Loneliness

- ☐ "I try to be optimistic, outgoing, and persevering."
- ☐ "I try to stop running away with bursts of activity and promiscuity. I try to understand the sadness. I've learned I can deal with these painful feelings. When faced head-on, they no longer devastate me. And if I deal with them, they become self-limiting."
- ☐ "I read something uplifting or inspiring."

- ☐ "I make a list of things to look forward to."
- ☐ "Exercise gives me a sense of well-being however my heart feels."
- ☐ "Writing letters gives me a sense of being connected to people."
- ☐ "I try to do something that will give me a feeling of accomplishment. I'll make something from a new recipe, clean a closet, wax the floor."
- ☐ "I am only lonely when I think I am."
- ☐ "I experience the sadness, sometimes with tears, and tough it out. These periods, thank goodness, pass."
- ☐ "I list all the negative points of my marriage. I read them out loud. I remember that I was often lonely when I was married. At least, by being single, I know I'm comfortable with me."
- ☐ "I don't fight or repress the sadness, but I also don't wallow in it. I try to find something funny to watch on TV."
- ☐ "If I feel teary, I cry and get it over with. When it's out, it's over."

In solitude you can dream your dreams, paint your pictures, and write your poems. You can talk to the wall, laugh out loud, and sing your songs. And you can remember.

I can close my eyes and see the terrace where I sat in California. I can visualize the blue of the water in front of me and the colored sails of the boats in the marina. When I pull this scene out of my memory, I feel at peace.

I can picture myself on one of those humid summer days in New York, being caught in a light rain and standing still—allowing the warm drops to wash over me, taking delight in the touch.

I can remember going cross-country by train and from my compartment watching the sun rise in Chicago. I can recreate the joy of that trip through imagining the scenery, which feels imprinted on my mind.

These scenes nourish my soul and feed my heart. They are a part of me, to be brought out when I'm feeling lonely.

Take some time right now to do your own remembering. Sit quietly and let the pictures come. Discard the ones that make you anxious. Focus on those that make you smile, that give you a feeling of warmth.

List key words, phrases, or sentences that will help you identify your pictures.

_____

_____

_____

_____

_____

_____

Personal Affirmations

A three-second quiz. What do self-esteem, self-confidence, self-worth, and self-fulfillment have in common? They all revolve around the self, and that's you!

Give yourself some pats on the back. You're not crying now; you're reading this book. You're trying new things, developing your interests, going out of your way to build a life. And you're trying to make that life as rich and full as you can—because it's the only one you'll ever have, and you can't afford to waste a minute of it.

List the five best things about being single.

_____

_____

_____

_____

_____

List five things you still want to change or need to work on.

_____

_____

_____

_____

_____

Study the first list when you're feeling blue. From time to time examine the second list. Note your progress. Can you cross out one of the lines? What do you still have to do to cross out the others?

Next, be conscious of the *should*'s and *ought to*'s that creep into your conversation. Stop yourself when you hear them. Do you really need to govern your life with rules? to bind yourself by responsibility? Do you always have to be the giver? the rescuer and nurse? Can you build a little self-love into your life? For instance, instead of the *should*'s and *ought to*'s begin to concentrate on your *want to*'s.

The four books I want to read.

_____

_____

_____

_____

The four letters I want to write.

_____

_____

_____

_____

The three foods I want to try.

_____

_____

_____

The three things I want to learn to do.

_____

_____

_____

The two people I want to know better.

_____

_____

The three activities I want to try.

_____

_____

_____

The four things I want to say to my best friend.

_____

_____

_____

_____

The two trips I want to take.

_____

_____

The three gifts to give to myself when I have the extra money.

_____

_____

_____

The one physical change I want to make in my appearance.

_____

The three things I want to accomplish by one year from today.

_____

_____

_____

Gaining Confidence

Write this affirmation on a piece of paper or index card and tape it to your bathroom mirror: *I am a strong, capable, competent, single woman.* Repeat it out loud every time you see it.

How do you begin to take those words to heart? to own them? You start by taking small steps in the area where you have the least amount of confidence.

You approach the goal in steps. For example, if Mary wanted to make a friend, she could (1) list the places or events she frequented or participated in with some regularity (work, health club, library discussion group, bridge club) and then (2) narrow the search (rule out work, "don't want to get too chummy or personal"; health club, "people too busy"; bridge club, "I already know the people"). Mary would then (3) attend a meeting of her library discussion group with the aim of exchanging phone numbers. Planning ahead, she'd (4) arrive at the meeting early and socialize. Before or after the discussion she'd (5) choose someone she'd like to see again and exchange numbers. The next day she could (6) call and arrange a meeting, having two dates and plans to offer.

And if the person was busy? Mary, persistent woman that she is, would try again a week later. If she is once more rebuffed, she'd let the other person make the next move. And Mary would try again with someone else.

No endeavor is guaranteed. The only thing you can do is try to get what you want, what will make you feel happy and better about yourself. Ignore the defeats. You have nothing to lose by trying some more. And on those days when your head says "Go" and your heart says "No," you've got to make that additional push. You've got to force yourself out the door. You're right, it's not easy. And life is not a daily diet of ice-cream cones.

The more new things you attempt, the greater your chance of success. With each small victory an adornment, you gain confidence. Imbibing the essence of your growing self-esteem, you're better able to accomplish larger goals.

Make your changes one day at a time. Applaud each venture out. Aspire for the sun, but settle for a star.

═══════════════

The Older Women's League (OWL) is a national organization addressing the special concerns of midlife and older women. There are eighty-seven chapters across the country.

Tish Sommers, the sixty-nine-year-old founder, has said, "We want to convey the message that older women have value, beauty, and significance. The last half of our lives can be the most active, vigorous, and vital." To this effort, OWL, like most women's organizations today, works toward changing the negative stereotypes and images of older women. In addition, the current national agenda focuses on six major issues facing women today. They are (1) Social Security, (2) pension rights, (3) health insurance, (4) caregiver support services, (5) jobs for older women, and (6) cuts in human services and entitlement budgets.

At monthly chapter meetings, members write letters to city and state officials on current legislation, speak out on topics of interest, and provide emotional and concrete support for one another. As a political advocacy group, OWL has its own Washington lobbyist. As a social network, friendships are formed and business connections expanded.

Dr. Ruby Benjamin is president of the Manhattan chapter of OWL.

"I'm fifty-three. This is what fifty-three looks like. This is what fifty-three feels like. I was a late bloomer. I'd dropped out of college and went back. It took me seventeen years to get my B.A. and five to get my doctorate. I was never so happy as when I was in school, learning and growing. I needed a role model.

And I'd say my analyst, who was a woman, fit the dish. She was divorced, but she'd just adopted a fine, healthy baby. And that just opened up a whole new world for me. You can do anything, almost anything, at every stage. There are some things I can't do. But there's a whole host of other things I can. If I can't do this, then I'll do that. And I still say I'm becoming.

"Working with OWL is my first encounter in politics. I never saw myself as a political person. And yet, I read, 'Advocacy is good for the soul.' It's wonderful to fight for yourself as well as for other women. It gives me a sense of personal and professional satisfaction. I'm making a contribution that's going to help me and, professionally, help others. The impact that OWL's had is because women have gotten together. They've advocated for change; they've testified; they've written letters. I used to say, 'What difference does it make if I write a letter?' I don't believe that anymore. At the drop of a hat, I write letters. And this is one of the things we do every month at our membership meetings. We write letters and we get responses. Women need to get involved, to educate themselves, to write the letters, to march, to support, to vote.

"On television, midlife and older people are portrayed as sick, victimized, bitchy, mean, and ugly. You rarely see an older woman with a younger man, always the other way. You see social relationships in the media. And where do you get your images from, other than your family? The media. The discrimination is pervasive.

"My consciousness has been raised. I'll give you a for-instance. I got a call the other day from a man with some travel agency. And he's talking to me. He's giving me this pitch. He'd like to talk to someone of importance, an officer. And I said, 'Why?' Because he's got this thing. He wants someone who's got power. I said, 'You're talking to the president.' Oh, he loved that! He gives me his pitch. Twenty percent off, you have to be over sixty, blah, blah. And I said to him, 'How much is the trip?' And he evaded the question and said something else, then 'darling.' And

I said, 'Wait a minute. Did I hear you say "darling"?' He said, 'Did I say something wrong?' I said, 'If I were a man, would you call me darling?' I said, 'I really consider this insulting, a put-down, a conde-scension. You don't know me from anything, and that's rather personal.' And he said, 'Oh, when you get to be a little older . . .' And I said, 'How old are you, thirty?' He said, 'No, forty-seven.' Then he ended something with "honey," and that did it. I said, 'I'm sorry, we're going to end this conversation. I find it very demeaning. I'm sorry. Thank you for calling.' And that's how we're discriminated against.

"I stood up. Women have to stand up. They have to be assertive without being nasty. They should say, 'I resent being called that.' If somebody calls us 'girls' or 'girlies,' I say, 'No, we're women. We're ladies.' I demand respect for my position in life and who I am.

"It's funny. I couldn't see myself at fifty. I didn't know what it meant, and here I am, beyond it. I don't know what sixty-five will be like because there are so many women that I know now who are vital and active at sixty-five that I hope that's what I'll continue to be. Several years ago someone asked me, 'What do you think you'll do in five years?' Well, I'd had a cancer operation, so I wasn't taking five years in advance. I was just taking it year by year. Now I feel I can plan for five years. What I want most is to be healthy and to take on life's opportunity, whatever it is. When I was in school, I wanted my doctorate. I wanted that so I could do the things I do in the health field and help people. I work better when I have a goal. And whether it's a short-term goal or a long-term goal, I like doing things and planning for them.

"Because of the cancer, I see things a lot differently now. What I considered important before, I don't consider as important now. So illness—serious illness, life-threatening illness—gave me a different per-spective on people and on things. I found I was caught up in a lot of perfectionism, seeking recogni-tion and being the best. That was important, going from position to position to position. It's not important anymore. Sure, I'd like to be rewarded for my work. I'd like to be recognized for what I do. But it's not the be-all and end-all of my life.

"I try to avoid stress. It's hard to do, and I don't always succeed. I think if you can recognize a stressful situation, one that's not good for you, you should try to get out of it, if it's at all possible. If it's not, seek professional help or support. Many times you get involved and can't see the alternatives. You're too much in the situation, too emotionally involved. Somebody who's objective can see things with a broader view. That person can put things in a different perspective. Or if you make the same mistake over and over, I think you should get some professional help to see why you're creating a destructive pattern that's not in your best self-interest. If it's an unconscious motivation, you're bound and compelled to do it again unless you find out why you're doing it. As a therapist, I try to help my patients work through their stress and destructive patterns. For me, it's terrific to see people grow and change.

"I like being single. I like my life. I have a number of good male and female friends. But I also like being by myself. I travel alone. I go to the theater alone. I don't let being alone stop me—from anything. I've learned to take care of myself."

For More Information

Books

Edwards, Marie, and Eleanor Hoover. *The Challenge of Being Single*. Los Angeles: J. P. Tarcher, 1974.

Peterson, Nancy. *Lives for Ourselves: Women Who Have Never Married*. New York: Putnam, 1981.

Shahan, Lynn. *Living Alone and Liking It*. Los Angeles: Stratford Press, 1981.

Sterns, Ann Kaiser. *Living Through Personal Crisis*. Chicago: Thomas More Press, 1984.

Yates, Martha. *Coping: A Survival Manual for Women Alone*. Englewood Cliffs, N.J.: Prentice-Hall, 1977.

3

Your Physical Self

I know we grow more lovely
Growing wise.

—Alice Corbin

Every once in a while it's good to take stock—to see where you've been and where you want to go, to unplug the stoppage and move on. You check the inventory of your kitchen shelves, probably without thinking. Why not take an inventory of your self?

How long have you been wearing your hair this way? When was the last time you bought a new color lipstick? Does your cologne still say waltz when you feel like disco dancing? Are your clothes outdated, a carry-over from another life? Do you need heels on your shoes or even a pair of new ones? If someone were to call right this minute and invite you to a concert, cocktail party, barbecue, or to the park, would you have something to wear?

When was the last time you stood nude in front of a full-length mirror and *really* looked at your figure? When did you last examine your face in the harsh light of the sun?

The time to take stock is *now*, and only you can do it.

Appearance

Are you satisfied with your appearance? Check yes or no.

Face	YES	NO	Body	YES	NO
Makeup	☐	☐	Weight	☐	☐
Eyes	☐	☐	Height	☐	☐
Eyebrows	☐	☐	Figure proportions	☐	☐
Eyelashes	☐	☐	Excess skin	☐	☐
Nose	☐	☐			
Mouth	☐	☐	**Clothes**		
Skin	☐	☐	Colors	☐	☐
			Styles	☐	☐
Hair			Coordination	☐	☐
Color	☐	☐			
Length	☐	☐			
Style	☐	☐			
Texture	☐	☐			

Look at your "no" answers. Learn to change what is fixable. Enhance what pleases. Make the most of *you!* For example, you won't be able to add inches, but you can learn to wear clothes to give the illusion of greater height. You can borrow books from the library on grooming, attend adult education courses on makeup, study the fashion magazines, ask advice from friends, and seek help from professionals.

Weight

There are moments when I'm convinced I was born a size fourteen. Over the years I've been (to my eyes) thin, overweight, and somewhere in between. I'm continually on diets, watching what I eat, and will most likely continue this pattern for the rest of my life.

I think the difference that has come with age is my attitude. I've given up the dream of being tall and slim (and of having long, straight blond hair). I find I like the look of my curves.

And I no longer go into a tailspin if I have a fat attack. Nor do I beat myself up for falling prey to a piece of strawberry cheesecake. When I fall off my diet wagon, I now enjoy my junk food without the guilt. I *allow* myself the treat because I know *I'm* in control, that I can stop. A candy bar today may mean cottage cheese tomorrow, but that's okay. Age has made me comfortable with my body. It has made me accept and be pleased by the way I look. It has made me realize and accept the days I'd like to hide under the covers because my hair won't cooperate or my dress won't zip. Those days come because I'm human. The nice thing is those days also pass.

Gerontologists at Duke University Center for the Study of Aging and Human Development cite obesity as one of the four reasons for premature aging. (The other three are inactivity, smoking, and the lack of life satisfaction.)

Obesity, most doctors conclude, just isn't healthy. People who are overweight are ripe for disease (for example, diabetes, gout, stroke, liver malfunctions, and high blood pressure).

You live alone. You don't like the way you look. You're overweight. Why? Is someone forcing you to eat? Are your cabinets filled with fattening treats? Do you eat between meals? Or does it go deeper?

Psychologist April Benson, an expert on eating disorders, believes women overeat for a variety of reasons. It might begin with the desire to fill an emptiness left by a childhood trauma. It might be to ameliorate current emotional problems involving loss (loss of love, children leaving home, loss of physical attractiveness, for example).

"Food and feelings about oneself are intricately linked," Dr. Benson stated. Sheri, sixty-one, agreed. Divorced a year, she admitted a weight gain of eighteen pounds. "I put up a wall of fat around me. I was left, and I don't want any other male coming close. I feel rotten, and I look rotten. Maybe when I feel better about myself, I'll begin a diet."

How can a woman break the eating cycle? I wanted to know. "The first step," Dr. Benson advised, "is to stop yourself in process. Watch what you're doing. Then move back to the feeling state. Ask yourself how you feel at this moment. Try to substitute another action for eating, one that's less self-destructive. Or you can call someone. Sometimes the verbalization takes the place of the compulsion to act."

Many women use their weight as a rationalization for the world's not living up to their expectations. "If I weren't fat," they say, "this wouldn't happen to me." You can also substitute descriptions such as *poor, thin,* or *gray-haired* for *fat*. The idea is you're giving up control of your life by using your status as a cop-out. Certainly discrimination exists. But how much of it is real, and how much is of your own doing?

Nancy Shapiro, a Chicago-based CSW (Certified Social Worker), is the founder of What You're Looking For Is Not in the Refrigerator. Working with individuals and groups, she maintains that "diets alone don't work because they're based on deprivation. Weight," Ms. Shapiro believes, "is carried on your body *and* in your head." With her clients, she uses a combination of diet, exercise, and an examination of the psychological issues that cause women to eat.

There are numerous ways to lose weight.

Weight Watchers is a twenty-one-year-old weight reduction program that includes a structured diet, group meetings, behavior modification techniques, and an exercise plan. Weight Watchers conducts approximately fifteen thousand classes a week all over the world. Classes are led by a Weight Watcher who has successfully maintained his or her goal weight. There is a fee for each class.

Overeaters Anonymous (OA) is patterned on Alcoholics Anonymous with members admitting they suffer from the disease of compulsive overeating. A 1981 survey found that 91.4 percent of the membership were women. Members try to abstain from overeating "one day at a time." A self-supporting organization, OA collects contributions rather than charging fees.

Both Weight Watchers and Overeaters Anonymous can be found in your local telephone directory.

This is it, folks. There's no way around it. If you eat more *calories* than your body can use, the excess is stored as fat. Let's say you're a moderately active woman. That would mean you need 15 calories per pound to maintain your weight. Say you want to remain at 140 pounds. That would mean you can consume no more than 2,100 calories worth of food each day (140 x 15 = 2,100).

To diet by counting calories, you must not only cut down on the amount of food you eat but also switch to those foods that are low in calories in order to get the proper nutrients. To lose one pound a week, you will need to eat 500 less calories *per day*. (The 140-pound woman from above? To diet, she will eat 1,600 calories a day. 2,100–500 = 1,600.)

If you combine exercise with a sensible diet plan, you will lose faster, become firmer, and look slimmer.

When your hand reaches for a cookie, change its direction.

Fruit	Approximate Calories
1 medium apple	76
1 small banana	85
1 medium orange	68
½ grapefruit	40
1 medium nectarine	32
1 medium peach	38
10 large strawberries	37
1 large tangerine	46

Food	Approximate Calories
1 boiled egg	77
1 dill pickle	11
4 large mushrooms	16
1 large artichoke	51
9 medium brussels sprouts	47
1 large stalk celery	7
1 cup plain popcorn	54
1 fried chicken drumstick	88

Can you say this five times quickly? Peanuts, pretzels, and potato chips put on pounds.

Many women try a *fast* at some time in their diet life. It can be done one day a week or one day a month. Converts to fasting cite benefits such as (1) a quick weight loss, (2) breaking a plateau period, (3) improved sleep, (4) loss of appetite, and (5) a feeling of tranquillity. When you fast, you can allow yourself black coffee, tea, bouillon, water, and diet soda. Do not begin a fast without your doctor's permission. Nausea, dizziness, or blurred vision are dramatic indications to resume eating. Break your fast with a small snack or a light meal.

Whatever diet plan you follow, do it with your good common sense.

How Other Women Handle Their Diet

□ "I don't eat after 8:00 P.M.

□ "When I have people in for dinner and serve something fattening—chips with drinks, dessert—I make sure that when my friends leave, the food leaves. Either they'll take home the leftovers or I'll dump them in the garbage. I don't want to be tempted."

□ "I love to read cookbooks, but that's all I do—read."

□ "I don't let my overindulgence get out of hand. I weigh myself every morning, and if I'm two pounds over my goal weight, I cut down on everything and completely cut out sweets."

□ "Since Weight Watchers, I take my own desserts—fruit salad, yogurt—to dinner parties. I let the hostess know in advance. There's never been any static, and I don't have to feel deprived."

☐ "I wash the kitchen floor after dinner and close the door. I don't enter again till breakfast."

☐ "When I indulge myself, I eat as much as I can and then immediately douse what's left in the kitchen sink. Waterlogged doughnuts quickly lose their appeal."

☐ "I try to be patient and realistic. I tell myself it took time to put on the pounds. It'll take more time to take them off."

☐ "I use specific diet foods whose calorie count is spelled out."

☐ "Water. Water-packed fruit and tuna, and straight up in a glass."

☐ "I write down everything I eat—even a piece of gum—in a small notebook I keep in my purse. The act of recording my food keeps me on my diet."

☐ "I weigh myself every Wednesday. If I've lost one pound or more, I buy myself an inexpensive treat— a flower, new nail polish, a sketch book."

☐ "I keep busy—too busy to think of eating between meals."

Try to keep a *food diary* for a week. Examine when, what, and why you put food in your mouth.

SATURDAY

Time	Food	When	Feeling
9:00 A.M.	orange juice whole wheat toast coffee	breakfast	
11:00	doughnut	coffee break	deserve it after cleaning the house
1:00 P.M.	tuna fish salad diet soda	lunch	virtuous, on diet
3:30	handful of peanuts		bored

SATURDAY (continued)

Time	Food	When	Feeling
6:00	broiled chicken salad gelatin coffee	dinner	good
8:15	diet soda cookies	watching TV	reward for being good at dinner— cookies in the house for my grandson
10:00	ice cream	on phone	angry with friend

What's going on? This woman plays her day like a yo-yo. She watches her food intake and feels good, then eats for emotional reasons—boredom, frustration, and anger. She uses food as a reward and to push down feelings. Sound familiar?

I'm *not* advocating for a society of women who are size ten. Losing weight will not guarantee a job, good health, a lover, or friendships. Only you can get those things. What I do encourage is for *you* to decide what weight makes you comfortable with yourself, what weight offers the greatest advantage to your overall health, and what weight makes you feel most attractive. It's your body, your health, your life. Take charge of it and be confident of your decision.

Posture

According to Marjorie Craig, a seventy-one-year-old exercise consultant and author, "Incorrect posture can be the cause of a protruding abdomen, thick waistline, sagging bust, protruding hips, stooped shoulders, double chin, short neck, knock-knees, bowlegs, and flat feet." Not a pretty picture!

Put this book down right now and go look at yourself in the mirror. Yes, right now. So how's *your* posture?

Bad habits of standing and walking develop over time. We practice poor posture without even being aware of what we're doing—until back or neck problems occur.

Susan L. Fish, a registered physical therapist, sees numerous women patients with problems resulting from poor posture. Go back to your mirror. Stand sideways. "Imagine a string," advises Ms. Fish, "as a straight line ideally going through your earlobe, shoulder joint, hip, knee, and ankle joint." Now face the mirror. "Think of yourself as a puppet with a string coming out of the back of your head, pulling you up." If you can carry that image with you, you'll begin to work on improving your posture. Also try to remember to pull in your stomach, raise your rib cage, and keep your chin parallel with the floor.

When you sit, Ms. Fish suggests you "sit up on your fanny, rather than sloping down on your lower back. A support, like a cushion, will help."

Skin

Posture, unfortunately, will not straighten out those wrinkles. Jo, sixty-seven, exclaimed with vehemence, "I don't plan on touching mine. I earned each and every one. Those lines are my life!" Wrinkles, however you feel about your own, are accelerated by exposure to the sun. Overexposure can result in brown, scaly patches on your face, arms, and hands. In addition, a study by the American Cancer Society indicates that too much sun may cause skin cancer (scary but usually curable when treated). The message seems clear that now is not the time in your life to become a bathing beauty. If you enjoy the sun, take precautions. Do wear a hat and use appropriate sun-block lotions.

Cosmetic Surgery

What improvements on your body can you make surgically? You can have a thigh lift, breast lift, face-lift (including chin and neck-muscle lift), eye lift, forehead lift, and buttock lift. In fact, a plastic surgeon can lift up almost anything that sags if you have the time, endurance, desire, and money.

Tanya, sixty-four, when asked about plastic surgery, replied, "You mean iron out my wrinkles? Look, I came into this world with this body. I hope to leave with it intact and unchanged, except through what it becomes through *my* efforts."

Lucille, seventy-three—who had her eyes, neck, and forehead done—disagreed. "Why shouldn't women look the best they can? If surgery can make me look better to myself, to feel good about my appearance, why shouldn't I nip and tuck if I can afford it? If the bottom line is putting on a good face for the world, I think I'm pretty lucky that in retirement I could make some adjustments."

According to Dr. Howard L. Gordon, Miami plastic surgeon, the patient who'll gain the most from cosmetic surgery will be the one who has realistic expectations, "the woman who wants not to look different, but to look better." Unrealistic expectations include having the surgery to please someone else, to find a lover/spouse, or to get a better job. "Realistically," Dr. Gordon added, "the surgery *can* make you feel better about yourself, more alert, more vigorous"—yes, folks—"even younger."

The three largest areas for cosmetic surgery in the country are New York, Miami, and Los Angeles. Prices vary in relation to the city in which you live and your choice of doctor: face-lift (lower face and upper neck), $2,000–$6,000; eyes, $1,000–$2,000; forehead, $1,000–$2,000.

You can choose a board-certified plastic surgeon, one who specializes in cosmetic surgery, from the following referral sources: (1) your local medical society and (2) a teaching hospital. Dr. Gordon suggested a third source, whom numerous women I talked to also recommended—your beautician. Sasha, fifty-two, told me, "The man who does my hair knows loads of women who've had it done. He's seen the results from the first after-surgery shampoo. He knows who does good work and whom to avoid."

————————

One woman's decision in favor of cosmetic surgery was an integral part of her determination to change her life.

Gretchen, fifty-five, is the vice-president of a public relations firm in a large midwestern city.

In the last year she made a number of far-reaching changes. She lost twenty-two pounds, asked her husband of twenty-four years to move out, and had a face-lift.

"My job has a great deal of visibility. How I look is important. After I lost all that weight, I became very self-conscious of the rolls of fat just hanging around, especially the folds of skin on my neck. I joined a health club and went to class four days a week. I majored in exercise and aerobic dancing. Certain parts of me got firmer. But I felt as if I didn't match. My body looked great, though my face screamed 'Older woman'!

"I went to my internist for a physical and asked him for a referral to a plastic surgeon. After I made the decision, I couldn't wait for the surgery. The only one I told was my sister. I planned the hospitalization—overnight—and recovery for my two-week Christmas vacation. My sister brought me home from the hospital and stayed at the apartment for the first week.

"The most uncomfortable part was learning to sleep on my side, not to disturb the bandages. Makeup covered the black-and-blue marks. The doctor removed the stitches after a few days, and my face was swollen for a few months. There was some numbness. But considering that I had major surgery, I feel as if I got off easy. [She did. Recuperation time will vary depending on type and texture of skin and what you have done.] I wanted the surgery too much to be fearful. I have my cheekbones back. I look more vital.

"This has been a year of personal inventory and decision making. My husband, a lawyer, is ten years my senior. He has gray hair and wears glasses and dentures. He was ready to retire to Florida and play golf for the rest of his life. I decided I wanted more. I still wanted the action. I wanted to continue to make decisions, to set policy, to become president of the company if possible. I'd worked too hard to get where I was. I wasn't ready, I felt, to get off the train.

"I married my husband when I was thirty-one. He'd been divorced and had three daughters who, at the time, lived in another state. Mike was smart, witty, sophisticated. He was the successful older man I needed to feel secure about myself." [Gretchen— tall, slim, auburn-haired, wearing a green silk dress, sitting behind a modern chrome and glass desk— appeared the picture of self-confidence. Her large corner office contained a conference table for eight and a sitting area with sofas and coffee table.]

"I needed Mike to tell me who I was, to define me as a woman. He became my champion, cheering each step I made up the corporate ladder and encouraging my growth and success. I think in the past few years our goals changed. Or rather his stopped; he'd reached his plateau. The sad fact of my growth is we no longer want the same things. He wants to rest—to stop making contacts, to never go to another fund-raiser. I want the lunches and dinners. I've been elected to a number of boards. I want the recognition

I've worked for. I no longer need Mike for definition. I *know* who I am.

"We parted friends. He's happy in his condo. And I'm getting used to being single. Aside from wanting the plastic surgery for my career, to give me a lift—that's a bad pun—I thought it would help me socially.

"Men my age are dating women the ages of my stepdaughters. Susie, the oldest, forty-two, brought someone over last week for drinks whom I knew casually through business. The truth is I was envious of her, resentful. I thought I'd be a better match—closer to his age, having more in common, more, well, suitable.

"I've only dated one man during the last nine months. He was my age and married, also in PR. We had three dates. I ended it. I kept thinking how I'd feel if Mike had played around. Although this man talked of a bad marriage, that didn't seem enough of an excuse. I don't want to be the 'other woman.' I want to be the *only* one.

"The best thing I took from this brief affair was sexual. I felt desired. As I undressed, I kept silently thanking the health club. I was terribly self-conscious, not so much about my body as what I would do in bed. Would I move right? Would I be acceptable? Would I be a good lover? When I went into the bathroom to brush my teeth, I looked in the mirror at my $4,000 face, newly colored hair, and slim figure and talked to my reflection. 'I'm an attractive woman,' I said. 'I'm bright. I'm nice to animals. I have a good sense of humor.' You see, I was so nervous I had to recite all my good points. And then I took a deep breath and said, 'Stop it. I'm going to enjoy myself with this man. I'm not alone in this. It takes two. Let *him* worry about pleasing me.' What happened after I finally left the bathroom was that we pleased each other.

"I don't think I want to remarry. I don't want someone there every night. I'm just beginning to feel relaxed by myself. I like coming home and not having to make conversation. I find I like the quiet. I'll make myself a simple dinner, read, listen to music, watch TV, or review something from the office. I don't have to worry about anyone but me, and, you know, that's quite pleasant.

"I'd eventually like a man in my life—someone who'd be there for me, when *I* needed *him*.

"While I've had moments of loneliness, I've also had moments of delight with women friends. As part of a couple, I tended to socialize with other couples. I still see friends as a couple, but now I see the difference. I'm the odd number, the third at a table for four. I also think I make my old friends uncomfortable. Mike and I were picture-album perfect. I'm sure some of them think I'm crazy—menopause madness—to give him up.

"Women friends—two in particular, single, around my age—have been terrific. I'm ashamed to say I didn't have enough time or energy when I was married to invest in outside relationships. My fault. We, the three musketeers, meet once a week for dinner, see a movie, go to a concert, or just talk. Last month they dragged me screaming to my first singles party. I hated it but knew they were nearby for support. I think I'm lucky I found them.

"Life is not a dress rehearsal. I've taken the necessary steps to ensure that the second half of mine will be a performance I'll never forget. Some women may think of my surgery as an indulgence. I prefer to view it as an investment."

Hair

There are other investments you can make in your physical appearance.

Ever want to be a sun-kissed blonde?

"Lightening my hair was comparable to going to a health spa. I felt rejuvenated," said Margaret, sixty.

A woman I know has spent years searching for the perfect haircut. She stops women on the street whose hair she likes and, after complimenting the look and style, asks for the name of their beautician and salon. Most women are flattered by her request, and she's never been turned down.

You can try this woman's technique. You can also define your face (for example, long, narrow, heart-shaped) and study the fashion magazines to see what looks good. Another option is to try on wigs in a department store.

Hairstyle and hair coloring can both add and/or subtract years and pounds and can make you feel different about yourself. (Ellie, sixty-nine: "For years I mourned the fact that I didn't have naturally curly hair. Last month I got a permanent. I don't know what took me so long. I *feel* different. I'm still gray. But now I'm curly gray, and that's given me a kind of perkiness, a feeling of freedom.")

Your aim should be to find a beautician who understands your lifestyle and who helps to make you look your best—one who does not interpret your aging as meaning you want a blue rinse and a set styling. (Renee, sixty-three: "I want to wash my hair, towel it dry, put on my clothes, and walk out of my house.")

Clothes

Emily Cho, founder of New Image, a personal fashion-consulting service, feels women should strive "to look appealing, to invite some exchange. Clothes show your attitude," she maintains. "They say how much responsibility you want to take, how open you are."

Do older women typecast themselves through their clothes? Ms. Cho believes they do by wearing "old lady colors" like brown and gray. "Dull," is her description. Instead, her advice is to wear "medium" colors—rose instead of red and teal blue in place of forest green. "Stay away from the 'baby colors,'" she suggests. "Pastels like baby blue and pink are passive."

In dress and makeup the key should be moderation and simplicity. "Nothing too extreme." For the woman over fifty the focus should be on *you!* Ms. Cho believes you should "celebrate who you are. You've arrived. You're special. Don't distract from that fact."

"Thin women," a friend who tries to maintain a weight of ninety-three pounds, complained, "are given short shrift." This is a woman who, when nervous or under pressure, stops eating. She too has difficulty in finding clothes. A size three or four, she purchases the tailored classics that are her trademark in the girls' department of a local department store. "Slacks and sweaters are no problem. Evening wear is a whole other dimension. I've found a couple of antique clothing shops that are great treasure troves for some dressier items. When I see something I like, I buy it whether I need it or not. I can never be certain I'll find what I need *when* I need it, so this stockpiling of clothing makes me feel more secure.

"I would never move to a hot climate," she confides. "I need the cold weather to wear my layers—turtleneck, shirt, cardigan—to look my best."

If you have difficulty with your size or with coordinating colors and styles, it's helpful to know a saleswoman at a store you frequent. Enlist her aid. Ask her to call when something comes in that might look good on you. Numerous department stores have personal shoppers. They will help you make the right selections. Call to make an appointment. Ask if there is a fee for the service. And don't be talked into buying anything you are not going to feel great wearing.

Do not overlook outlet and discount stores for your clothing needs. Such stores often offer large selections of good clothes at lower prices than other retail establishments.

Take a clothing inventory. What do you need right now? What can be put off? Check your newspaper for store sales and holiday specials (May, lingerie and handbags; October, furs; and so on).

CLOTHING INVENTORY

Shoes

dress   _buy navy blue high heels_

slippers   _____

sandals (sport and dress)   _____

sneakers   _____

boots   _____

walking   _____

Lingerie and Hosiery

panties   _____

bras   _____

girdles   _____

panty hose   _____

stockings   _____

slips   _____

Basics

skirts   _____

blouses   _____

T-shirts   _____

sweaters   _____

slacks   _____

blazers   _____

dresses   _____

suits   _____

Outerwear

hats   _____

scarves   _____

gloves   _____

coats   _____

jackets   _____

rainwear   _____

umbrella   _____

Additional Items

_____   _____

_____   _____

You live with your appearance on a daily basis. Why not take the time to take stock and implement the changes that will make you feel better about yourself?

For More Information

Organizations

Weight Watchers International
800 Community Drive
Manhasset, NY 11030
(*Weight Watchers Magazine*
 available at newsstands.)

Overeaters Anonymous
World Service Office
2190 190th Street
Torrance, CA 90505

Many women have successfully lost weight and kept off pounds through programs offered by the Diet Workshop, the Diet Center, and Nutri/System. Consult your telephone directory for locations. Before enrolling in any weight-loss program, check with your doctor. Also investigate the claims of the program. Determine whether the program is nutritionally sound for your physical health and whether you will be able to incorporate the diet into your lifestyle.

Publications

BBW (Big Beautiful Woman). A magazine for the large-sized woman. Published bimonthly. Available at newsstands or from Suite 214, 5535 Balboa Boulevard, Encino, CA 91316.

50 Plus Magazine's Guide to Health . . . and your retirement. (Write to "50 Plus," Whitney Communications, 850 Third Avenue, New York, NY 10022 for information on this and other publications.)

Weight Loss (free booklet from the Food and Drug Administration). Send postcard to Consumer Information Center, Department 81, Pueblo, CO 81009.

Calorie counters (palm-sized booklets usually available near the checkout counter at your supermarket). Invest in a collection.

Books

Cho, Emily, and Hermine Lueders. *Looking, Working, Living Terrific 24 Hours a Day.* New York: Ballantine Books, 1983.

Craig, Marjorie. *Miss Craig's 21-Day Shape-up Program.* New York: Random House, 1968.

LeShan, Eda. *Winning the Losing Battle.* New York: Bantam Books, 1981.

Nudel, Adele. *For the Woman Over 50.* New York: Taplinger Publishing Co., 1978.

Orbach, Susie. *Fat Is a Feminist Issue.* New York: Berkley Publishing Corp., 1979.

Pinkham, Mary Ellen. *Mary Ellen's Help Yourself Diet Plan.* New York: St. Martin's Press, 1983.

Schrader, Constance. *Nine to Five: A Complete Looks, Clothes and Personality Handbook for the Working Woman.* Englewood Cliffs, N.J.: Prentice-Hall, 1981.

4

Health Needs

Tell yourself that you do not stop being yourself, even when caught in a helpless state. The medical care you get can do only part of the job of helping you recover. The other half is staying in charge of your life.

—Eda LeShan

When my body is out of kilter, be it with a cold or a torn ligament, then I too am out of kilter. I find myself becoming cranky. I'm easily upset and have a low tolerance for frustration. The fact is I feel I'm not running on all four burners, and my work and social life suffer. Therefore, it's to my advantage to take the necessary steps to ensure my good health. Since *your* health and *your* view of the world are linked, to keep it all spinning depends on *your* vigilance.

Preventive Care

As a single woman, *you* are the *only one* responsible for your health care. Only you know when there's discomfort, where there's pain, and whether something feels different. You are the only one who recognizes a lump, a bump, or a bruise that wasn't there the day before or that's been there too long. Although being sick is sometimes scary, ignoring the signs that something is wrong can be even worse.

The good news is that you've passed the time for measles, mumps, mononucleosis, and chicken pox. The bad news is that, as an older woman, you get the chance to be knocked down by osteoporosis, heart disease, hypertension, arthritis, diabetes, and cancer. (And these are just the diseases with the most publicity.) Don't get carried away by the names or symptoms or what your overactive imagination screens for you at four in the morning.

If you *know* your body, you'll be able to get help when the unusual occurs. (Suzanne, fifty-nine, has a history of *never* running a temperature. "When, if ever, it's two degrees above normal, you can bet I'll be in my doctor's office within the hour.")

When to See a Doctor

☐ appearance of blood in the urine or bowels
☐ persistent diarrhea or constipation
☐ a noticeable, unexplained weight change (either gain or loss)
☐ a series of dizzy or fainting spells
☐ a persistent pain in any part of your body
☐ an unquenchable thirst or any burning sensation during urination
☐ a nagging cough or hoarseness
☐ a change in size or discoloration of a wart or mole
☐ any unexplained symptom that is incompatible with your usual good health

It is important to have your health team in place *before* you need them. Choosing the people who'll be responsible for your life, for the wellness of your body, is, to me, among the most important decisions you'll ever make. If you don't have such a team, call friends and get recommendations or call your local hospital and ask for a referral.

After you've collected a few names, you become

Brenda Starr, investigative reporter. Call the doctor's office and interview the nurse.

1. Training. Where did the doctor go to medical school? Is the school one with a good reputation?
2. Certification. Is the doctor certified? A board-certified physician had to pass a written and oral examination and has had an approved hospital residency.
3. Affiliation. At what hospital does the doctor have privileges? (A teaching hospital is preferable because of staffing and equipment.) In case there's an emergency, can you get to the hospital quickly?
4. Experience. How long has the doctor been in practice?
5. Location. Can you reach the doctor's office quickly and easily?
6. Hours. Are the hours compatible with your free ones?
7. Cost. Are the fees within your budget or covered by medical insurance? Does the doctor accept Medicare assignment?
8. Gut-level reaction. What is the nurse's tone? Does she or he sound friendly? Is she or he abrupt without an apology? Can the nurse answer all your questions to your satisfaction? Does the nurse suggest another time for you to call so that she or he can answer your questions without interruption?

Later, if your first visit is reassuring, that's great. You can now let someone else share your physical worries. If, however, the treatment or attitude of the doctor does not meet your expectations, find a different doctor. (Remember, *you're* the only one who's experiencing the pain—the only one who will know when you are symptom-free.)

The American Cancer Society suggests an annual physical examination. This includes the taking of a

medical history (with any presenting problems) to be
followed by the examination of the following:
- □ skin
- □ head and neck (mouth, nose, throat, eyes, ears)
- □ chest (including X ray)
- □ abdomen
- □ colon and rectum
- □ blood
- □ urine
- □ breast
- □ pelvis

Your doctor will most likely tailor your exam,
adding or subtracting tests to meet your individual
needs.

Emergency Care

Let's say it's now three in the morning and you've been
lying awake, in pain, for the past hour. ("Why is it,"
asked Virgie, fifty-nine, "that the big pains never
come during business hours?") You can call a friend or
relative to relieve your anxiety. You can try to reach
your doctor. You can hope it will pass. Or you can go
to the nearest hospital's emergency room. Dr. Steven
Greenberg, affiliated with Columbia Presbyterian
Medical Center, suggested the following guidelines
for a visit to the ER.

Go to the hospital
—if you're too sick to wait to see your regular doctor.
—if you've been in an accident.
—if you experience chest pain.
—if you have severe abdominal pain.
—if you have difficulty breathing.
—if you vomit blood.
—if you have a temporary loss of consciousness.

If you go, it's good to have a friend either take you or
meet you there. (If you are in pain, it may not be wise

for you to drive alone.) Negotiating any system can be difficult, but negotiating your own health care when you are frightened and in pain may only increase your discomfort. A friend can speak for you when you may be too ill. He or she can give information, listen for instructions, and lend emotional support.

Forget about how wonderfully self-sufficient and independent you usually are. *Now* you need help. Ask for it!

Gynecologist

There used to be the good old reliable family doctor, the general practitioner who treated *all* of you. Now there are doctors who treat specific parts of your body. If necessary, your primary care physician (this can be an internist) will recommend you to a specialist (for example, if you have muscle strains or pains, fracture a bone, or dislocate a joint, you may be referred to an orthopedist).

One specialist, known as the "woman's doctor," is the gynecologist. Many women feel self-conscious when they make their semiannual or annual visit. It's hard to relax with a stranger (usually a male) examining your sexual organs.

To minimize your discomfort, you should be given something with which to cover yourself (a gown or a sheet). You also have the right to have a nurse in the room with you during the examination.

The doctor should examine your breasts for any unusual lumps or growths. (Ask to be shown how to do this procedure yourself—see pages 52-53.) An internal, or pelvic, exam is performed to feel the size, shape, texture, and mobility of your uterus. Many doctors also perform a yearly Pap test for detection of cervical cancer. In addition, the Pap smear can pick up signs of infection and reveal the status of your hormones.

How to Examine Your Breasts

(This is a *must* for women of all ages.)

1. In the shower:

Examine your breasts during bath or shower; hands glide easier over wet skin. Fingers flat, move gently over every part of each breast. Use right hand to examine left breast, left hand for right breast. Check for any lump, hard knot or thickening.

2. Before a mirror:

Inspect your breasts with arms at your sides. Next, raise your arms high overhead. Look for any changes in contour of each breast, a swelling, dimpling of skin or changes in the nipple.

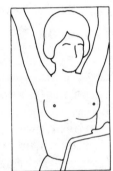

Then, rest palms on hips and press down firmly to flex your chest muscles. Left and right breast will not exactly match—few women's breasts do.

Regular inspection shows what is normal for you and will give you confidence in your examination.

3. Lying down:

To examine your right breast, put a pillow or folded towel under your right shoulder. Place right hand behind your head—this distributes breast tissue more evenly on the chest. With left hand, fingers flat, press gently in small circular motions around an imaginary clock face. Begin at outermost top of your right breast for 12 o'clock, then move to 1 o'clock, and so on around the circle back to 12. A ridge of firm tissue in the lower curve of each breast is normal.

Then move in an inch, toward the nipple, keep circling to examine *every part of your breast,* including nipple. This requires at least three more circles. Now slowly repeat procedure on your left breast with a pillow under your left shoulder and left hand behind head. Notice how your breast structure feels.

Finally, squeeze the nipple of each breast gently between thumb and index finger. Any discharge, clear or bloody, should be reported to your doctor immediately.

Why you should examine your breasts monthly

Most breast cancers are first discovered by women themselves. Since breast cancers found early and treated promptly have excellent chances for cure, learning how to examine your breasts properly can help save your life. Use the simple 3-step breast self-examination (BSE) procedure shown here.

For the best time to examine your breasts:

Follow the same procedure once a month about a week after your period, when breasts are usually not tender or swollen. After menopause, check breasts on the first day of each month. After hysterectomy, check your doctor or clinic for an appropriate time of the month. Doing BSE will give you monthly peace of mind and seeing your doctor once a year will reassure you there is nothing wrong.

What you should do if you find a lump or thickening

If a lump or dimple or discharge is discovered during BSE, it is important to see your doctor as soon as possible. Don't be frightened. Most breast lumps or changes are not cancer, but only your doctor can make the diagnosis.

On the following lines post the dates of your breast self-examination.

_____   _____
_____   _____
_____   _____   _____
_____   _____
_____   _____
_____   _____

You should be able to share your concerns and ask your doctor questions about sexual activity, menopause, estrogen replacement therapy, any discharge, vaginal bleeding or pain, and any thickening in your breasts. If the doctor dismisses your complaints with "It's only your age," you need to find a new doctor.

Since this examination is so intimate, it is important that you feel comfortable with your doctor's manner, attitude, and availability. If you don't, you must find someone else whom you can trust and who will put you at ease.

Foot Care

When you think of your overall health, how often do you think of your feet? Your feet contain 25 percent of your body's bones. The ball of your foot receives 60 percent of your body's weight. A normally active woman takes 7,000–8,000 steps per day. A study conducted by the Pennsylvania College of Podiatric Medicine found the average American walks 115,000 miles (the equivalent of more than four times around the world) in a lifetime.

These are pretty important facts concerning an area of the body we sometimes take for granted. We shouldn't. Consider that the feet usually age faster than the rest of the body, since they are the farthest from the heart. Circulation deteriorates with age. As a result, all the structures lose their elasticity, skin becomes drier, the foot pad becomes thinner, the joints become stiff and lose some motion, and the toenails become hard and brittle.

Aside from these disorders, can you honestly say you've never complained of aching feet? If the ache doesn't go away and you "could have danced all night" but didn't, then maybe it's time to consult a podiatrist.

A podiatrist has four years of undergraduate training and four years at podiatry school. There is also a one-year residency or internship program. He or she is then granted a DPM (Doctor of Podiatric Medicine) degree. Podiatrists are licensed by the state to diagnose and treat problems involving the foot—to perform surgery, prescribe medication, and take X rays.

A typical initial visit (usually more extensive than subsequent visits) might include the following steps: The podiatrist will take a full medical history of problems pertaining to general foot health, including but not limited to diabetes, circulation, and surgery on any part of the body. Sometimes problems affecting the body influence the feet. The podiatrist will inquire about medication being taken, allergies to medicine, and who the patient's medical doctor is. Finally, the doctor will inquire in depth about the presenting problem (how it started; when it started; the type of pain, if any, the patient experiences).

A whirlpool soak (approximately ten minutes) is occasionally used. Its only purpose is for the patient's immediate comfort. It may relax tired muscles but generally does not facilitate treatment.

The examination concentrates on, but is not limited to, the problem that brought the patient to the podiatrist. The doctor will also note the look and feel of the skin, test circulation, and check motion of the joints.

If the doctor feels the problem involves interior structures of the foot—joints, bones, or deep tissue—an X ray will be taken. The dosage of a podiatric X ray is extremely low, as it is directed far from the center of the body. A lead shield, though, should be worn as an extra precaution.

A diagnosis can generally be made based on the information obtained from the medical history, physical examination, and X ray. Problems of the foot range from the simplest, thickened nails, to the most complex, bunions or joint problems.

A person with no pain or symptoms should visit a podiatrist once a year for a routine foot checkup. If you experience recurring corns or calluses, you might want treatment as frequently as every six to eight weeks. An average visit will last from twenty to thirty minutes, depending on the problem.

If you can't reach a podiatrist immediately, there are some simple home measures you can take. For an irritation from a shoe, commercially purchased pads of moleskin or lamb's wool can provide relief. For pain of a superficial infection, soak the foot in luke-warm water to which you have added two teaspoons of table salt. For an injury, ice is the best treatment. Apply ten to fifteen minutes on, ten to fifteen minutes off, for about an hour and a half.

Care of Teeth

Working upward, how's your smile? It doesn't have to follow that the addition of years results in a subtraction of teeth *if* you've been taking care of them.

Periodontal disease (gum decay, bone loss) appears to be the major threat to women over fifty. (Periodontal disease can also be a cause of bad breath. How to tell if you've got *it*? Breathe on your fingers. Now smell your hand.)

If your gums appear red and swollen or if they bleed easily when you brush your teeth, you need to see a dentist immediately.

According to the American Dental Association (ADA), the word *periodontal* comes from two Greek words that mean "around the tooth." Periodontal disease attacks the gums, bone, and other structures that hold the teeth in the jaw. If untreated, it can destroy the bony support of the teeth. The teeth will then become loose. Eventually, they may fall out or have to be removed.

Some cases can be treated by a dental hygienist, who will thoroughly scale the plaque (colorless film of bacteria) and tartar (buildup of plaque along the gum line that turns into a hard deposit). For more advanced cases, a visit to a periodontist may be suggested.

In the ADA booklet *How to Be a Wise Dental Consumer,* the following recommendations are made to locate a qualified dentist in your area.

- Call your dental society.
- Speak to your family physician or local pharmacist.
- Ask friends, neighbors, or co-workers for a referral.
- Speak to faculty members of local dental schools.
- Call a hospital that has an accredited dental service.
- Check the ADA directory in your public library.

The key to staying out of dental trouble is prevention. You must learn to take care of yourself *before* your health care turns into an emergency situation.

You should see your dentist every six months for a checkup and cleaning.

A full set of X rays should be taken every three to four years, on the average. You should be covered by a lead shield during any X-ray treatment.

Ask your dentist to recommend a toothbrush specifically for your teeth and mouth. Toothbrushes should be replaced approximately every three to four months.

Dental floss is to be used to get at the places your toothbrush can't reach—under the gum line and between the teeth. You should floss every day.

Maintain a balanced diet. Keep consumption of sugar to a minimum.

"I told my daughter that when I die, I want my teeth, all my teeth, to be in my mouth," said Marion, seventy.

More than fifty million Americans wear dentures. The alternative, being toothless, is not a terribly attractive option. Having teeth is not just for the sake of appearance. Your ability to chew food will be improved as will your speech.

It is to your advantage if your dentist can save a few healthy teeth for a partial denture. If not, full dentures may be necessary. Since this procedure is an extensive one, it is important that you trust your dentist, obtain as much information as you can, and faithfully follow all instructions on wear and care.

Eye Care

You may be able to replace your teeth. It's not so easy with your eyes. Who is in charge here? An ophthalmologist is a medical doctor qualified to diagnose and treat diseases of the eye. An optometrist can examine your eyes and prescribe appropriate therapy (glasses, contact lenses, referral to an ophthalmologist). An optician is a specialist qualified to fill the ophthalmologist's or optometrist's prescription for lenses.

Glaucoma and cataracts are the two major concerns for women over fifty. Dr. Alan Robins of the American Academy of Ophthalmology said in an interview, "More than 90 percent of the people who are ultimately found to have glaucoma are unaware of it because its first symptoms—a gradual loss of side vision—occur so slowly they go unnoticed." Simply put, glaucoma is pressure that builds up within the eye. Normal fluid drainage is blocked. In acute cases there is blurred vision, pain, and redness. The individual may also see halos around lights. Glaucoma is often hereditary. It *can* be treated and controlled with drugs or surgery.

A cataract is a progressive clouding of the lens. It sometimes occurs with women who are diabetic. Symptoms include trouble seeing detail, fuzzy or double vision, and seeing better in twilight than in daylight or in bright light.

When there is increased loss of vision, surgery is indicated. First the cataract is removed, and then a new lens is inserted. This implant operation has become relatively pain-free. The hospital stay is usually overnight. Vision is restored in 95 percent of the surgical cases.

Serious eye problems leading to blindness can be prevented. Do have an eye examination every year or two. (Some community service agencies will do it for free.) If you've been given a prescription for glasses, have them made and wear them! Or you might choose contact lenses. Read in the proper light. And use a magnifying glass for small print. Don't strain your eyes. They're all you've got!

Evaluation of Medical Treatment

My criteria for good medical treatment (for me) has evolved over the years.

If I'm addressed as "Jane," I address my doctor by his or her first name.

I always call approximately an hour ahead of my appointment to see whether the doctor is on schedule. This saves needless waiting at the office when I could be doing something else. I generally expect fifteen minutes or so overlap. But if I have to wait on more than one occasion for over thirty minutes without an explanation or an apology, I scratch this doctor off my list. To me, this seems reflective of the doctor's attitude toward patients, toward organization of the office, and toward how the doctor sees himself or herself. I simply believe my time is as valuable as the doctor's.

Although I feel like a five-year-old when I'm ill, I don't expect to be treated like one when I see my doctor, nor do I want surprises during the examination. I want to know what is being done to me and why. I want to know what the doctor finds and what the results mean. And I want a clear explanation of how my treatment plan, if needed, is chosen. I find it's helpful for me to take notes. (Louisa, sixty-five, brings along her tape recorder. "I don't want to miss a thing," she said.)

If I call the office, I expect to be called back. The doctor-patient relationship is a professional one, and I respect it. If I call, I don't want a chat but an answer to a question or a clarification of some aspect of my treatment. To save the doctor's time, I make a list of questions or symptoms before I place the call and keep it by the telephone.

I realize that good medical treatment is more than a matter of etiquette. Yet I don't think it is improper to demand that along with competence my diagnostician demonstrate some degree of humanity. I am more than the sum of my bodily parts, and I expect that to be taken into consideration.

Hospitalization

Consider this scene. You are in your doctor's office. You've been examined. You're now sitting across the desk from the doctor, and he or she recommends surgery. You gulp and take a deep breath while the doctor stresses that it's *not* an emergency (gallbladder operation, hernia, hysterectomy, perhaps).

After your stomach settles down, you need to get your head and mouth working. Now is the time to get information.

The U.S. Department of Health and Human Services suggests that you know the answers to the following questions before agreeing to any nonemergency surgery.

☐ What does the doctor say is the matter with you?
☐ What is the operation the doctor plans to do?
☐ What benefits would ensue as a result of the operation?
☐ What are the risks of the surgery, and how likely is it that they would occur?
☐ How long would the recovery period be, and what would be involved?
☐ Are there any possible side effects to be considered?
☐ What would be the costs of the operation? Would your insurance cover all of those costs?

☐ What will happen if you don't have the operation?
☐ Are there other ways to treat your condition that could be tried first?

If a delay won't be harmful to your health, get a second opinion. This isn't disloyalty; it's good common sense. It's also required by some insurance companies. You can do any of the following:

☐ Ask your doctor for the name of another doctor.
☐ Call your local medical school or teaching hospital for a referral to a specialist.
☐ Call the federal government's toll-free number, 800-638-6833, for a referral.
☐ If you are covered by Medicare, call your local Social Security office.
☐ If you are eligible for Medicaid, call your local welfare office.

A second opinion will help you obtain as much information as possible in order to make the correct decision regarding your surgery. Isn't your health worth the additional time and effort?

If you find yourself a patient in the emergency room or in the hospital proper, professional support is available in addition to the medical staff.

The patient representative for ambulatory care at St. Luke's–Roosevelt Hospital Center, Marjorie Krug, described her responsibilities in the emergency room. "The patient representative offers emotional support to the patient and family members. She ensures that the patient's rights are respected and provides the patient with mechanisms through which she can seek solutions to the problems she encounters."

There are approximately three thousand patient representatives, or patient advocates, employed in hospitals across the country. They function both in the emergency room and on patient floors. Wherever they are, their goal is the same—to look at the problem or situation from the patient's viewpoint. It can be a problem as simple as having the phone in your room repaired to interceding on your behalf with the dietician.

And every hospital has a Department of Social Service. Staffed by social workers, the department usually seeks out high-priority cases for visitation (for example, kidney dialysis, coronary care). Yet it doesn't matter *why* you're admitted, because "everyone" said Lois Orlin, CSW, assistant director of social work at St. Luke's–Roosevelt, "is entitled to their services." What can they do for *you?*

Clinically trained, they can provide reassurance if one needs to talk, explain medical tests and procedures, offer information on health insurance and benefits, discuss discharge planning (will you need a homemaker or visiting nurse when you leave?), meet with your family and/or children, and interpret your needs to the medical staff.

"All a patient has to do," continued Ms. Orlin, "is pick up the phone and ask for us."

Being hospitalized is never easy, physically or emotionally. But the patient representative and social service staff are on *your* side. Use them!

The Patient's Bill of Rights is a document that attempts to establish a code of professional courtesy and ethical conduct.

Patient's Bill of Rights*

The American Hospital Association presents a Patient's Bill of Rights with the expectation that observance of these rights will contribute to more effective patient care and greater satisfaction for the patient, his physician, and the hospital organization. Further, the Association presents these rights in the expectation that they will be supported by the hospital on behalf of its patients, as an integral part of the healing process. It is recognized that a personal relationship between the physician and the patient is essential for the provision of proper medical care. The traditional physician-patient relationship takes on a new dimension when care is rendered within an organizational structure. Legal precedent has established that the institution itself also has a responsibility to the patient. It is in recognition of these factors that these rights are affirmed.

1. The patient has the right to considerate and respectful care.

2. The patient has the right to obtain from his physician complete current information concerning his diagnosis, treatment, and prognosis in terms the patient can be reasonably expected to understand. When it is not medically advisable to give such information to the patient, the information should be made available to an appropriate person in his behalf. He has the right to know by name, the physician responsible for coordinating his care.

3. The patient has the right to receive from his physician information necessary to give informed consent prior to the start of any procedure and/or treatment. Except in emergencies, such information for informed consent should include but not necessarily be limited to the specific procedure and/or treatment, the medically significant risks involved, and the probable duration of incapacitation. Where medically significant alternatives for care or treatment exist, or when the patient requests information concerning medical alternatives, the patient has the right to such information. The patient also has the right to know the name of the person responsible for the procedures and/or treatment.

4. The patient has the right to refuse treatment to the extent permitted by law, and to be informed of the medical consequences of his action.

5. The patient has the right to every consideration of his privacy concerning his own medical care program. Case discussion, consultation, examination, and treatment are confidential and should be conducted discreetly. Those not directly involved in his

care must have the permission of the patient to be present.

6. The patient has the right to expect that all communications and records pertaining to his care should be treated as confidential.

7. The patient has the right to expect that within its capacity a hospital must make reasonable response to the request of a patient for services. The hospital must provide evaluation, service, and/or referral as indicated by the urgency of the case. When medically permissible a patient may be transferred to another facility only after he has received complete information and explanation concerning the needs for and alternatives to such a transfer. The institution to which the patient is to be transferred must first have accepted the patient for transfer.

8. The patient has the right to obtain information as to any relationship of his hospital to other health care and educational institutions insofar as his care is concerned. The patient has the right to obtain information as to the existence of any professional relationships among individuals, by name, who are treating him.

9. The patient has the right to be advised if the hospital proposes to engage in or perform human experimentation affecting his care or treatment. The patient has the right to refuse to participate in such research projects.

10. The patient has the right to expect reasonable continuity of care. He has the right to know in advance what appointment times and physicians are available and where. The patient has the right to expect that the hospital will provide a mechanism whereby he is informed by his physician or a delegate of the physician of the patient's continuing health care requirements following discharge.

11. The patient has the right to examine and receive an explanation of his bill regardless of source of payment.

12. The patient has the right to know what hospital rules and regulations apply to his conduct as a patient.

No catalogue of rights can guarantee for the patient the kind of treatment he has a right to expect. A hospital has many functions to perform, including the prevention and treatment of disease, the education of both health professionals and patients, and the conduct of clinical research. All these activities must be conducted with an overriding concern for the patient, and, above all, the recognition of his dignity as a human being. Success in achieving this recognition assures success in the defense of the rights of the patient.

This list is basically consistent throughout the country, though additional points may be added according to the individual state's Department of Health. You should receive a copy when you enter the hospital. If you don't, ask for one.

Remember: *Maintaining good health is your responsibility. Obtaining good health care is your right.*

Do visitors help or hinder your recovery? Well, it depends. Brenda, fifty-seven, hospitalized for five days for tests and then released, commented on her visitors: "I wasn't feeling well to begin with. Then all those tests were a further assault on my body. I was wiped out. All I wanted was to be left alone—to sleep, to regroup my strength. While I adore my friends, their chatter was just too much, at that time. It would have been better for me if they had held their visits till after I'd gone home. *Then* I could have used the diversion."

Abigail, sixty-four, had a different experience: "My visitors kept my mind off of *me*. I'd been sick for over a month before I went into the hospital. I knew I was getting the best possible medical care. I wasn't worried about that. Waiting out the treatment was the only agony. My friends, though, pulled me through. They literally baby-sat me from the beginning to the end of visiting hours. If it hadn't been for them—their gossip and games and hand holding—I honestly believe my recovery wouldn't have been so successful."

If you're the patient, you have to decide what will help in your recuperation. Is total rest, or peace and quiet, what's needed? Or would a little company, a little diversion, speed the healing process?

If you're the visitor and your friend, the patient, wants company, consider these points.

□ Call ahead to see when would be a good time to come (so you don't interrupt any tests or treatment procedures).

□ Keep your visit under thirty minutes unless the patient asks you to stay longer.

□ Do not sit on the bed.

□ Share your concern, but not your fears.

If you choose to visit, you may want to bring a gift, something other than the traditional flowers. What about these?

□ a cotton nightgown (The cotton ones absorb perspiration.)

□ dry shampoo

□ a large hand mirror

□ a small transistor radio with earplug

□ a book rack

□ goodies—if they are allowed (fruit, cookies, cheesecake, pizza, Chinese food)

□ notepaper and stamps, a packet of postcards

□ room freshener

□ small crossword-puzzle books

□ an assortment of small change—dimes and quarters— for your friend to use for newspapers or for items from the gift shop.

□ a small stuffed animal for "companionship"

□ making a prepaid appointment for her to be visited by the hospital's beautician for a wash and set (Check with the doctor first.)

If *you* are the patient and you do not want to be disturbed, yet have a hard time saying no to potential visitors, you can enlist the aid of the nursing staff. Inform them of your decision. Let them be responsible. You do not have to feel guilty if you are doing something in your best interest.

At-Home Health Care

I know a woman who is so organized that her medicine cabinet is arranged in alphabetical order. True (aspirin, burn ointment, epsom salts)! Yours doesn't have to be, but when was the last time you checked the contents?

Melanie, seventy-five, writes the date on each nonprescription item she buys. *Her* shelf life is a year; then she throws the item out.

The following checklist consists of suggestions. *You* know best how your body runs and what items you'll need on hand for that occasional tune-up.

Item	On Hand
aspirin	☐
antacid	☐
antiseptic solution	☐
peroxide	☐
epsom salts	☐
burn ointment	☐
petroleum jelly	☐
cough syrup	☐
antidiarrhetic	☐
adhesive bandages	☐
sterile gauze pads	☐
oral thermometer	☐
absorbent cotton	☐
eyecup	☐
scissors	☐
tweezers	☐
heating pad	☐
ice bag	☐
hot-water bottle	☐
vaporizer or humidifier	☐
elastic bandage	☐

It is a good idea to check the medicine cabinet periodically to see what you need to replenish or what you need to throw out.

You should also own a first-aid manual and keep it where it's most accessible. (An aunt of mine keeps one in the kitchen, on a shelf that holds her cookbooks.)

Now make up an index card with the following information.

Care Provider	Telephone Number
Doctor	_____
Neighbor	_____
Fire Department	_____
Police Department	_____
Nearest Hospital	_____
Ambulance Service	_____
Pharmacist	_____

You can make copies and post them around your house. (Place on refrigerator, by bed, by phone.)

It is also a good idea to have a list of any special allergies or ailments and the names of the prescribed medications you may be taking for these conditions. You could tape this list to the inside of the medicine chest.

Drugs

Make the neighborhood pharmacist your friend. No, I'm not kidding! A licensed pharmacist, bachelor of science degree in pharmaceutical studies, must have passed a five-year course of study and a three-day state exam. As the link between patient and doctor, he or she has the time and information necessary to aid in your treatment. In addition to filling prescriptions, the pharmacist can also make recommendations on necessary over-the-counter preparations (for example, vitamins, antacids, eye drops, and health and beauty aids).

Pharmacist Eugene Dong drew up the following questions for you to ask when picking up a new prescription: (1) When should medication be taken? (2) Should medication be taken before or after meals? (3) What are the adverse reactions or possible side effects? (4) Are there any contraindications with any other medication I am taking? (5) Should this medication be refrigerated?

I think the pharmacist must be considered a member of your health team. Here's someone you don't have to have an appointment to see!

A further word on drugs. Overmedication is a growing problem. Women don't have to shoot up in back alleys. Some women are legally abusing drugs with prescriptions from their friendly physicians.

An estimated one-third of all hospital admissions are related to complications caused by drug therapy. Approximately two million American women wind up as victims.

One doctor prescribes a tranquilizer (for example, Valium) for anxiety attacks. Another prescribes a painkiller (for example, Darvon) for a bad back. A third prescribes a sleeping pill (for example, Dalmane) for insomnia. In addition, a woman may be taking diuretics, hormones, and vitamin and mineral supplements.

Mood elevators, or antidepressants (for example, Elavil, Sinequan, and Tofranil), may not only be addictive but can also cause physical symptoms such as drowsiness, blurred vision, vertigo, and muscular incoordination.

Drugs are chemicals. When indicated, they are powerful and beneficial. However, while they relieve the target symptoms, in interaction they may create an adverse complex of symptoms. Any side effect from the use of a new drug—any interference with your day-to-day functioning—must be reported to your doctor. He or she can then reevaluate the risks and potential benefits.

Keep an up-to-date list of all the medications you are taking. If your doctor suggests adding or subtracting a drug, present the list for reexamination.

Do not increase or decrease your medication without first consulting your doctor!

What happens with some drugs is the development of both a physical and a psychological dependency. A tolerance is quickly established (as with amphetamines, "uppers"), and progressively larger doses are required. Withdrawal symptoms (fatigue and depression) may sometimes feel more unpleasant than the original need.

If you are unable to stop taking or to reduce your use of a drug, if you find you need a higher dosage to get the same effects, if your daily functioning is becoming impaired, or if friends express concern, you may be on the road to addiction.

If you believe you are overly dependent on drugs, take heart. There is help available throughout the United States in more than nine thousand treatment programs for chemical dependence. Most major hospitals have a detoxification unit and a therapy regimen. Referrals can also be made to outpatient groups and to individual counselors.

If Elizabeth Taylor and former First Lady Betty Ford can admit to drug-related problems and go for help, so can you!

Alcoholism

Another substance that has been abused is alcohol. And the disease that can kill you, which you have the power to stop, is alcoholism.

—————————

Ruth, sixty-two, said, "I was a social drinker when I was married—a drink with my husband when he came home from the office, wine with dinner, a nightcap before we went to bed. Alcohol gave me a nice, warm, comfortable feeling. He had a drink; I had a drink. It was something we shared."

When her husband left her for another woman after thirty-five years of marriage, she reported being "devastated."

"The children were out of the house. We were financially comfortable. I felt we were entering a wonderful new period in our lives. The divorce cut me off at the knees. It was a blow to my self-esteem. And I guess old habits become ingrained. Some nights I had a drink before dinner, and some nights I just skipped dinner entirely. I was filled with anger and resentment. I was so ashamed to be with our friends, at least the ones he hadn't seduced away, that I just hid in the house. Food wasn't important. Children weren't important. The nighttime drinks were not even giving me importance. I started to think that if two stopped my jangled nerves, three or more would really calm me down.

"A part of me realized that I couldn't stay home forever, however embarrassed I was to be left, so I started meeting women friends for lunch. And a drink became my appetizer. Drinking was no longer a choice; it was a need. I really despised what I was becoming but felt powerless to halt my decline.

"One evening I volunteered to baby-sit for my daughter. When she returned home, I was passed out on the living-room sofa, a bottle on the floor and the baby wet and howling under the coffee table. My daughter was furious. I was humiliated. The next day she called to say that I wouldn't be left alone with the baby—that she wouldn't trust me until I went to a meeting of Alcoholics Anonymous. She convinced me to go with her to an open meeting. And then she began to go to Al-Anon, a support group for families and friends of alcoholics while I attended AA.

"That was four years ago. And I realized that being an alcoholic didn't cure the hurt, the sadness, or the loneliness. Only I, myself, could do that."

The American Medical Association and the United States Public Health Service agree that alcoholism is a complex disease involving medical, psychological, and social factors.

In a nationwide survey of twenty-five thousand members of Alcoholics Anonymous, 31.8 percent of the respondents were women aged fifty and over.

The National Council on Alcoholism cites a population of ten million alcoholics, one-third to one-half of whom are women. There may, in fact, be many more—hidden away at home, alone, and too guilty or ashamed to seek help.

On the other hand, women do not have to fit the "bag lady" stereotype to be alcoholics. Many women who have a drinking problem are well-groomed, sociable, responsible members of the community.

Vera Lindbeck, author of the article "The Woman Alcoholic: A Review of the Literature," states that "female alcoholics begin to drink at a later age, and the transition from controlled to uncontrolled drinking is more rapid than for male alcoholics."

And Lois Lester, CSW, notes the different perceptions of male and female alcoholics: "Unfortunately for most women who drink, society maintains a double standard: social drinking is acceptable; intoxication is not. The intoxicated male is either treated with indifference, perceived as amusing, or pitied for his drunkenness. In contrast, the intoxicated female is often scorned and held in contempt for her drunken behavior."

Do You Have a Drinking Problem?

- ☐ Do you have "blank" periods when you can't remember your actions?
- ☐ Has anyone commented on the quantity of liquor you consume?
- ☐ Do you feel that drinking makes you more sociable?
- ☐ Are you using alcohol to anesthetize your feelings?

- Are you disgusted by your drinking and feel out of control?
- Has your appearance changed?
- Do you lie to others about your drinking?
- Do you need to have a morning drink to "get you going"?
- Are you preoccupied with when you'll have your next drink?

The most widely recognized program for men and women able to admit they are "powerless over alcohol" is Alcoholics Anonymous. By not drinking "one day at a time," sobriety is maintained through the support and example of other members, a conscious working through of the Twelve Steps Program, and attendance at group meetings.

Membership in AA is voluntary. There are no fees or dues. And anonymity is guaranteed. (For information and/or a referral to a meeting, look up Alcoholics Anonymous in your telephone book.)

Women for Sobriety was formed in 1975 by Dr. Jean Kirkpatrick, a recovered alcoholic, who believed women needed a self-help program different from that used by men. With Thirteen Statements of Acceptance as basic guidelines, women learn to turn their negative feelings (powerlessness and loneliness) into positive affirmations of themselves and their lives. In a sense, who better to understand your past and present than other women who have traveled similar roads?

WFS groups are small (eight to ten women). The meeting, usually held once a week, is led by a recovered alcoholic and is focused on a particular topic of concern to women. Donations are requested to cover expenses.

WFS may be used as an alternative to, or in conjunction with, AA.

Other options for treatment include hospital detoxification programs, mental health clinics, and individual therapy with qualified professional counselors.

Smoking

Tobacco might also be considered another abused substance when we recognize the widespread publicity given to the dangers of smoking. Medical evidence cites a direct correlation between smoking and lung cancer, heart disease, and respiratory illness. In addition, it has been found that smoking causes more wrinkles than outdoor exposure. If you are addicted to nicotine, consider this choice: to be free of the smoking habit or to participate actively in your own destruction. There are organized groups and various methods to help you break the smoking habit. Wouldn't it make you feel better to look better? to be free? to reach for a carrot instead of a cigarette?

Physical Fitness

Some women feel that they get enough exercise just getting out of bed in the morning. Some have incorporated specific organized activity into their daily lives. Others have recently become converts to movement through the jogging craze. And still others are just waiting for the right moment (next week, next month) to get into their sweat pants. Where do you fit?

It used to be we didn' have to work at exercise. We were younger then and more active. Working around the house meant reaching, stretching, bending, pushing—moving. Now, while laborsaving devices continually make things easier, they also cut down on our need for movement. (You can press a button from your bedside rather than get up to switch the channel on your TV!)

If you feel it's time to firm up and flatten down, the first requirement for joining any kind of exercise program (your own or someone else's) is your doctor's consent. Bad knees? A problem back? What will strengthen rather than strain? What can you do? What should you avoid? Do you have the stamina for aerobics? the feet to be a runner?

The buzzword is *moderation*. Whatever you choose to do, begin s-l-o-w-l-y and build up gradually. Work at your own pace.

Nora Braverman, YMCA (Young Men's Christian Association) physical fitness and yoga teacher, advised, "The key is to start now. Don't put it off any longer. Make the decision today."

The choice of exercise and/or apparatus to use can be somewhat overwhelming. For example:

Walking. This is one of the all-time best natural exercises. Try to increase the amount and/or the distance. (Lorraine, fifty-eight: "If it's too cold or too late to walk outside, I walk up and down the hallway in my apartment house.")

Running. This exercise works your lower body. You can do it anywhere. You'll most likely do stretching exercises to warm up before running and to cool down afterward.

Swimming. This exercise works all the major muscle groups. In addition to the physical benefits, swimming can be an aid to the relief of tension and anxiety.

Aerobic dancing. This is usually performed with music. You stretch, skip, kick, leap, and dance. This type of exercise strengthens the heart, increases the rate of blood movement, and tones the large muscle groups.

Isometrics. These are static exercises that pit one muscle group against another. It is a way to tone and tighten specific parts of your body.

Hatha-yoga. This is an age-old system of physical exercise and controlled breathing. It is a set of standard exercises to stretch the body. (Marilyn, seventy-six: "I've tried a number of exercise classes over the years, but I always think of yoga as being the most gentle on my body and mind.")

Rowing machine. This apparatus works the whole body, with no stress on the joints. The exercise is self-paced and both burns up calories and builds up stamina. (The machine can be folded up and stored in a closet.)

Stationary bicycle. Use of this apparatus strengthens your cardiovascular system. It works only your legs.

Weights. These are braceletlike tubes that fasten around the wrists and ankles. Muscles must cope with the additional load as they contract and extend in movement. The effect of the exercise is intensified. A suggested beginner weight is two pounds on each limb. (Dumbbell-type weights are good for arm development.)

Whatever you decide to do, choose something that won't become a chore.

Some women can work through a standard set of exercises, alone, faithfully, day after day. Then there's Alicia, sixty-one: "I need a group. I need a teacher who will count for me, 'Hold it; one, two, three. Now breathe out.' When I pay the fee, it's my hard-earned money going for my self-improvement. I feel obligated to show up for class."

Exercising in a group can help your motivation. Four women over seventy in Pasadena, California, meet five mornings a week at 7:30 to walk around their neighborhood. They cover from three to four miles a day.

Exercise classes can be held in a friend's apartment, in a community center, at the local high school, at the neighborhood Y, or in a health club. (Numerous condominiums in Florida, for instance, have exercise classes in their daily activities program.)

Ask to visit a class before you sign up. Note the number of students and the amount of room. Is there enough space? Note the quality of instruction. Does the teacher move around the room? Is she encouraging? Does she help individual students? Is the class paced too fast? too slow? Are the people enjoying themselves?

Workout clothes can be a leotard and tights or old

pants and a sweat shirt. You don't want to wear anything that will restrict your movements. Remove dangling earrings and long necklaces.

Recommended exercise times vary. Some instructors urge two fifty-minute classes a week. Others suggest a daily thirty-minute workout. Do what fits into *your* schedule and what makes *you* feel good.

If you feel dizzy or nauseated, if your legs shake and your head pounds—*stop!* The exercise may be too difficult for you at *this* time. The old slogan No Pain, No Gain is a lie. Exercise teachers now believe that if a movement gives you pain, you are doing something wrong or that the movement may be unsuitable.

And by all means, try to integrate exercise into your day-to-day life. Walk instead of taking transportation. When you're watching television, work in some leg lifts. While you're in line, jog in place. As dinner cooks, do some arm circles.

Ms. Braverman extolled the positive effects of exercise as (1) decreased risk of circulatory problems, (2) strengthening of bones, (3) improved posture, (4) control of weight, (5) more restful sleep, (6) a better sexual response, and (7) an overall sense of well-being.

Choose one of the following activities and begin to *move those muscles!*

aerobics	miniature golf
ballet	running
bicycle riding	skiing
boating	swimming
bowling	tennis
folk dancing	walking
gardening	waterskiing
golf	yoga

Phyllis lives in a one-bedroom apartment in a suburb of Chicago. At fifty-eight, she is five feet two inches and weighs 107 pounds. Her black curly hair is shoulder length.

Phyllis was married at twenty and became the typical suburban mother of two. She excelled at golf, sculpture, car pools, and volunteer work.

Describing her husband, she said, "He was the first man who asked, so I said yes. Six months later I realized I should have said no. Divorce was simply unheard of in my day. I stayed in the marriage but felt like a prisoner." During the last eight years of her twenty-year marriage, she was celibate. Her husband was a nice, simple man whom "I grew to hate. I spent the years in limbo, waiting for the other shoe to drop. It finally did when he asked for a divorce. On one hand I was ashamed that I'd somehow failed, yet there was also a feeling of liberation."

Phyllis met her second husband, a man ten years her senior, at a cocktail party. "He was exciting, seductive. He lived on the edge. He did everything in excess, and I felt like a bird who'd suddenly been uncaged. It was ten years of heaven and hell. He was the love of my life, and he was an alcoholic.

"Unfortunately, the greatest symptom of alcoholism is denial. I denied it because what it meant was that I had chosen somebody who was a sick, disturbed person. I couldn't face up to that—that this was a decision I had made.

"It's only recently we understand it's a disease. I had to be hit over the head by almost getting killed in a car accident before I was able to admit that he and I *both* had a problem.

"I found I was quarreling with my children. I was pushing my children away from me. I was isolating myself from relatives, from friends. And I knew my life was changing, radically.

"He worked. He made a good living, and he drank. I would make sure that I was always home by the time he came home; no matter what I was doing, I'd be home to be with him. And I'd watch him till he passed out. He was physically and verbally abusive. He was a victim of the bottle; I was a victim of him.

"We were in a terrible accident. We were both almost killed. I got out of the car, and I said to him, 'Why don't you call the police?' And he said, 'Because I was drunk.'

"Stan and I went to a psychiatrist, and she said, 'Without question, Stan is an alcoholic.' That's the first time I'd heard the word applied to my husband. And she said to me, 'You go to Al-Anon.'

"When I got out of the car and I was still alive, I felt that I had another chance at life and that I was going to make the most of it.

"I had six years at Al-Anon. Al-Anon was a means of exploring one's inner self because if you live with an alcoholic, you're living very much alone—he's in a stupor. So what are you going to do? Where are your resources? They have to come from within. I continued to go to Al-Anon for a year after Stan died of a heart attack. It was a refuge.

"They diagnosed my multiple sclerosis when I was in my midforties. When I first had my attack, I had double vision, and my limbs were affected. You can't feel things. If you slip on glass, you might not know it because your feet are numb. So that was the first year. Most of those things disappeared, though they went back and forth over the years. The only thing I was left with was loss of control of my anus. I'm incontinent.

"But I feel that the mind and body work together, and I can and do control it. I tell myself I don't want to be embarrassed. I don't want to have an accident.

"I can't do anything that's going to let me get weak. If I'm tired, then I know I'll have problems with my bowels. So I know I have to keep myself in as good physical condition as I can. I swim. I started taking swimming lessons when I was fifty-four. I never swam before. My diet is such that it's very healthy. I eat no fat. I ride a bicycle regularly. I do more things than most women my age do but not because I want to be different; I want to be well. I'm aware that I have to take care of myself. Most people don't have to worry about stuff like that. The better I am, the happier I get, the more I want to do. And it's just wonderful.

"I've found I'm not as frightened as I used to be because of a new scooter I've found. It's for invalids who are handicapped and can't get around. It's a scooter, and you can actually wheel it into a restaurant, and it looks like a regular chair. Open up the front and it looks like you're sitting at a table. When I saw somebody in that scooter, something happened to me, and I was no longer as afraid of getting an attack as I used to be.

"I'm very philosophical about it. Everybody has something. And this is very little, considering how much damage there could have been.

"I've been fortunate in terms of money. I saved everything I got from both husbands. I read books, took seminars, and found an honest stockbroker. I probably study the market as intensely as he does. When I invest, I want to be damn sure I know where my money's going.

"I think that one has to take from within oneself. You have to satisfy your own needs. I think you have to depend on your own resources and trust yourself. You have to try new things. You have to experiment with yourself. You have to see what you like, what you don't like.

"Since I've been widowed (six years), I've traveled to India, Brazil, Italy, and Paris. I've gone to a dude ranch and a health spa, and I've gone hot-air ballooning—alone. I'm the woman I always wanted to be—my own. I think my illness has made me more adventurous.

"I take a lot of adult ed courses. I'm back to my sculpture. I go to the theater and the ballet. I do volunteer work two days a week.

"Sure, I get lonely. But there were times when I was lonely with each of my husbands. If I get lonely now, I'll call someone or go somewhere. I refuse to sit with it and get depressed. I'm alive. My disease is in remission. What more could I ask for?

"I went into therapy two months ago to gain further insight into myself. I want to learn to use every part of me that's well.

"It's wonderful to have a mate to share things with. Maybe I'll remarry in my seventies. But I don't think that's really the answer. I think it comes from within."

For More Information

Organizations

The following organizations offer a variety of services. They may provide information, do peer-group counseling, or make referrals for treatment in your area.

Epilepsy Foundation
4351 Garden City Drive
Landover, MD 20785

Muscular Dystrophy
   Association
810 Seventh Avenue
New York, NY 10019

National High Blood
   Pressure Information
   Center
120/80 National Institutes
   of Health
Bethesda, MD 20014

Reach to Recovery
777 Third Avenue
New York, NY 10017
(for women who have had
   mastectomies)

Make Today Count
PO Box 303
Burlington, IA 52601
(for persons with cancer
   and their families)

Leukemia Society of
   America
211 East 43rd Street
New York, NY 10017

Soroptimist International of
   the Americas
1616 Walnut Street
Philadelphia, PA 19103
(has project on impaired
   hearing)

National Association for the
   Deaf
814 Thayer Avenue
Silver Springs, MD 20910

National Multiple Sclerosis
   Society
205 East 42nd Street
New York, NY 10017

National Society for the
   Prevention of Blindness
79 Madison Avenue
New York, NY 10016

AA General Service Office
Box 459
Grand Central Station
New York, NY 10163
(for books, pamphlets)

Women for Sobriety
Box 618
Quakertown, PA 18951
215-536-8026

Organizations (continued)

The Arthritis Foundation
3400 Peachtree Road, NE
Atlanta, GA 30326

National Foundation for
  Ileitis and Colitis
295 Madison Avenue
New York, NY

Office for Handicapped
  Individuals
U.S. Department of Health
  and Human Services
200 Independence Avenue,
  SW, Room 338D
Washington, DC 20201

United Ostomy Association
1111 Wilshire Boulevard
Los Angeles, CA 90017

Mended Hearts, Inc.
721 Huntington Avenue
Boston, MA 02115
(for recovered heart
  surgery patients)

National Association of
  Patients on Hemodialysis
  and Transplantation
505 Northern Boulevard
Great Neck, NY 11021

Publications

Thinking of Having Surgery? Surgery, HHS, Washington,
DC 20201

Food and Drug Interactions by Phyllis Lehmann (HHS
Publication II [FDA] 81-3070). Office of Public Affairs, HHS,
Food and Drug Administration, 5600 Fishers Lane, Rock-
ville, MD 20857

Medic Alert. Medic Alert Foundation International, PO Box
1009, Turlock, CA 95381-1009. ("One in five Americans has
a medical condition that should be immediately known in
an emergency. The Medic Alert emblem [necklace or
bracelet] speaks for you—when you cannot.")

A variety of leaflets concerning dental health: periodontal
disease, diet, dentures, bridges, and crowns. Bureau of
Health Education & Audiovisual Services, American Dental
Association, 211 East Chicago Avenue, Chicago, IL 60611

Using Your Medicines Wisely: A Guide for the Elderly.
Elder-Ed, PO Box 416, Kensington, MD 20795

Information and tips on how to stop smoking can be
obtained through your local branches of the American
Cancer Society, the National Tuberculosis Association, and
the American Heart Association. You can also write to
Action on Smoking and Health (ASH), PO Box 19556,
Washington, DC 20006, and to Narcotics Education, Inc.,
Box 4390, Washington, DC 20012.

Toll-free Hotlines

Better Hearing Institute. Provides information about hearing loss and help available in your area regarding doctors, hearing-aid specialists, etc. (800-424-8576)

Cancer Information Services. Offers information about all aspects of cancer. (800-4-CANCER)

National Health Information Clearinghouse. An information and referral service for health and disease-related questions. (800-336-4797)

Books

On Health

Annan, George J. *The Rights of Hospital Patients.* New York: E. P. Dutton, 1975.

Barkas, J. L. *The Help Book.* New York: Charles Scribner's Sons, 1979.

The Boston Women's Health Collective. *Our Bodies, Ourselves.* New York: Simon & Schuster, 1976.

Brody, Jane. *Jane Brody's Guide to Personal Health.* New York: Avon Books, 1982.

Kirkpatrick, Jean. *Turnabout: Help for a New Life.* New York: Doubleday & Co., 1978.

Mindell, Earl. *Earl Mindell's Pill Bible.* New York: Bantam Books, 1984.

Porcino, Jane. *Growing Older, Getting Better.* Reading, Mass.: Addison-Wesley Publishing Co., 1983.

Verby, John, M.D., and Jane Verby. *How to Talk to Doctors.* New York: Arco Publishing, 1977.

On Physical Fitness

Fiore, Evelyn. *The YWCA Way to Physical Fitness: How to Make What You Have Better.* New York: Doubleday & Co., 1983.

Frankel, Lawrence J., and Betty Byrd Richard. *Be Alive As Long As You Live: The Older Person's Complete Guide to Exercise for Joyful Living.* New York: J. B. Lippincott Co., 1980.

Marx, Gilda. *Body by Gilda.* New York: Putnam Publishing Group, 1984.

Books (continued)

Rowen, Lillian, and D. S. Laiken. *Speedwalking, the Exercise Alternative.* New York: Putnam Publishing Group, 1980.

Solomon, Henry, M.D. *The Exercise Myth.* New York: Harcourt Brace Jovanovich, 1984.

Wood, Peter D. *Run to Health.* New York: Charter Books, 1980.

5

Emotional Well-Being

*God grant me the serenity
To accept the things I cannot change;
The courage to change the things I can;
And the wisdom to know the difference.*

—Anonymous

Dr. Mildred Schwartz, a psychologist in private practice and the director of treatment at the Institute for Contemporary Psychotherapy, defines emotional good health as "being yourself and being comfortable with that."

Among the special problems she sees for older women are loss of youthful appearance, the empty-nest syndrome, the feeling of never being able to find another mate, anger at peer-age men dating and marrying younger women, parents aging and dying, limitations in job and career, and the beginning of physical problems such as high blood pressure. These are some of the issues related to aging that must be worked through and handled. These are some of the issues that produce stress.

Stress

What is stress? It is a physical or psychological strain. What may be stress for one person is merely a challenge to another. We have all learned different levels of stress tolerance based on how we have handled difficult situations in the past.

Will the stress in your life make you sick? The following quiz was developed by T. H. Holmes and R. H. Rahe and called "The Social Readjustment Rating Scale." Take a few minutes to fill it out.

What has happened to you during the past year? Read the list of life events below. When an event applies to you, jot down the point value for that event in the adjacent blank. When you reach the end of the list, add up your score.

A score less than 150 indicates a mild problem with a 30 percent chance you will feel the impact of stress with physical symptoms. From 150 to 299, you qualify as having a moderate problem with a 50 percent chance of experiencing a change in health. A score of over 300 gives you an 80 percent chance of becoming ill.

Life Event	Point Value	Your Score
Death of spouse	100	_____
Divorce	73	_____
Marital separation	65	_____
Jail term	63	_____
Death of close family member	63	_____
Personal injury or illness	53	_____
Tired of work	47	_____
Marital reconciliation	45	_____
Retirement	45	_____
Change in health of family member	44	_____
Sex difficulties	39	_____
Gain of new family member	39	_____
Business readjustment	39	_____
Change in financial state	38	_____
Death of close friend	37	_____
Change to different line of work	36	_____
Mortgage over $30,000	31	_____
Foreclosure of mortgage or loan	30	_____

Change in responsibilities at work	29	_____
Son or daughter leaving home	29	_____
Trouble with in-laws	29	_____
Outstanding personal achievement	28	_____
Begin or end school	26	_____
Change in living conditions	25	_____
Revision of personal habits	24	_____
Trouble with boss	23	_____
Change in work hours or conditions	20	_____
Change in residence	20	_____
Change in recreation	19	_____
Change in church activities	19	_____
Change in social activities	18	_____
Mortgage or loan less than $30,000	17	_____
Change in sleeping habits	16	_____
Change in number of family get-togethers	15	_____
Change in eating habits	15	_____
Vacation	13	_____
Christmas	12	_____
Minor violations of the law	11	_____

Total Score   _____

Professionals in the mental health field are beginning to recognize the stress inherent in the "sandwich generation." These adults (perhaps you?), sandwiched between their aging parents and their own maturing children, are being faced with an unexpected array of emotional and financial concerns. Professor Dorothy Miller of the University of Kentucky, Lexington, described the conflict this way: "They are ready for relaxation and self-indulgence, only to find that their grown children are not quite independent and their parents have moved from autonomy to a degree of dependence."

Interestingly enough, it is usually the woman, the daughter, who is called upon to take charge, to be responsible.

If the responsibilities and demands get out of hand, emotional support becomes a necessity.

People handle stress in various ways. Some salivate at a new, seemingly impossible project and thrive under the pressure. Others? A friend can't stand to wait, be it at the checkout counter or in a doctor's office. Another's teeth are set on edge as soon as she arrives at a party. A third woman becomes anxious when she knows she'll see her daughter-in-law. When your adrenaline starts pumping, your reaction may be commonly thought of as fight (deal with threat) or flight (evade threat). It's the necessary physical preparation for action.

In addition, some women I've talked to report physical symptoms when under stress, such as diarrhea, headaches, back pain, asthma attacks, and jangled nerves.

What can you do? *Don't drown your stress in alcohol or sedate it with drugs.* First, try to be aware of your stress periods. Observe what happens to your body. Are your shoulders hunched? Are you grinding your teeth? Are your palms sweaty or your hands cold? Does your neck feel tight? Are you sighing? Consciously try to either change the event or your reaction to it.

For example, focus on only one problem at a time and consider all options. Think of a situation where you are under stress. What can you do to reduce the stress? Can you walk away? Can you delegate responsibility? Can you find another way to deal with the situation or the person? Can you have someone accompany you or intercede in your behalf?

And if you continue to feel stressed, do one or more of the following:

Breathe deeply.	Buy something for yourself.
Take a walk.	Write down how you feel.
Exercise.	Talk to someone.
Clean your floors.	Meditate.

"Meditation," notes writer Bette Ziegler, "is a non-toxic compound that automatically reduces stress."

When you meditate, your heart rate, oxygen intake, and breathing slow down. This contributes to positive physical health.

Ms. Ziegler adds, "One of the greatest benefits of meditation is the heightened overall sense of well-being after one has been meditating regularly." It appears cyclical. When people feel good about themselves, they are able to cope. If they feel capable of coping, this helps them reduce the stress in their lives. What do you have to lose?

The following exercise was developed by Dr. Herbert Benson from Harvard University. It is a beginning meditation that Ms. Ziegler uses with her students.

The first thing to do is find a quiet place where you won't be disturbed. It is preferable to do the meditation two to three hours before or after eating. (If you are home, you can time your meditation period on your oven timer.) Then follow these suggestions.

1. Sit in a comfortable position.
2. Close your eyes.
3. Keep your back straight.
4. Beginning at your feet, progressing to your face, relax your muscles.
5. Breathe through your nose.
6. Become aware of your normal pace of breathing.
7. On each out breath say the word *one* silently to yourself.
8. Continue the in-and-out pattern for ten to twenty minutes.
9. Try not to dwell on any distractions.
10. When finished, sit quietly for a few moments with your eyes closed. Open your eyes. Remain in place for a few more moments.

If you are interested in taking a class in meditation, check your local community, adult education, or yoga center.

Sometimes, after a crisis or stressful encounter, you may experience a *panic attack* that seems overwhelming. If you were to list all the objects and situations that cause people to feel tense, anxious, and fearful, you would probably need a stack of paper. For example, some people experience difficulty when they are exposed to storms, heights, open spaces, animals, or insects. Others may be troubled by speaking in public or meeting new people.

The term *phobia* is used to describe the behavior of a person who actively avoids the object or situation that upsets him or her. Let's say JoAnne has a phobia regarding elevators. She is so fearful (phobic) about taking one that she chooses to walk up the stairs to whatever her destination. If JoAnne lives in an area of skyscrapers, her phobia becomes a problem.

Phobic reactions vary and can resemble an acute anxiety attack. They are often physiological: You feel dizzy. You perspire. You hyperventilate. They may also be observable: You turn and run. You freeze. You avoid the object or situation. The phobia becomes unmanageable when it interferes with your daily functioning.

You may understand and even be able to discuss the past experiences leading to your phobia (when JoAnne was younger, she got stuck in an elevator). You can try to gradually desensitize yourself through repeated encounters with the particular subject of the phobia. For example, JoAnne might ask a friend to stand in the elevator with her while it was at ground level. On another occasion, she might ride up one floor and walk down. On a third visit, she might walk up three flights and take the elevator down. Over time, JoAnne's fear would diminish as she learned to tolerate her anxiety, subdue her feelings of panic, and achieve a measure of comfort.

There is available help for phobias and panic attacks. Treatment methods include individual and group therapy with specially trained counselors and/ or participation in phobia clinics associated with hospitals and medical centers.

Friends as Support

A thesaurus lists the following synonyms for friend: *neighbor, well-wisher, alter ego, bosom buddy, partner, associate, ally, chum, pal, playmate, companion, intimate,* and *confidante.* Whatever the word or whatever the degree of closeness, a friend can help you deal with stress, depression, loneliness, and the problems of living—if you let her.

Take some time to think about your friends, to think about friendship. What changes an acquaintance to a friend?

"When I told her I hated her and she didn't believe me." (Janet, sixty-seven.)

"She made it a point to call every day between four and five for a whole month. She knew that was my low time after my husband died, and she was there for me." (Lucille, seventy-one.)

"She doesn't tell me when I've gained weight. My mirror can do that!" (Ruth, fifty-three.)

"When she goes to the library for herself, if she sees something I'd like, she'll take it out." (Aleatha, sixty.)

"I truly believe that my happiness is as important to her as hers is." (Pearl, fifty-five.)

"Honesty. When she thinks I'm wrong, she tells me, with gentleness." (Lisa, sixty-eight.)

"She's the only friend who makes me laugh—the kind of silly laughter that's eye-tearing and body-aching." (Donna, fifty-nine.)

"I can be utterly stupid, foolish, and uncaring, and she'd still accept me." (Tony, seventy-four.)

I have different friends for different reasons. One pushes me to be more outspoken, applauding when I break the rules or stand up for others or buck the bureaucracy. Another supports my quiet side, listening to the poet in me while we aimlessly walk the city streets exploring themes of life and love. And a third is the rock—the friend who bundles me up and takes me to the emergency room, who is unfailingly there through the good times and the bad, and who has grown along with me, yet remains separate and distinct.

Each of these women complements something in myself. Hopefully, I do the same for them.

I don't take friendship lightly. I think it takes energy to sustain. And as flowers need watering, friendship needs nurturing. There will be moments when someone gets on your nerves or says or does something unkind, insulting, even thoughtless. And it hurts. Perhaps you keep your distance for a while. You let the situation cool off. And then maybe you need to deal with what happened, to get back on track in a new way. For instance, "I felt hurt when you said . . ." Or, "I need to talk about what went on last week. I'm feeling very uncomfortable." Whatever words you use, the important thing is to clear the air and let go of the hurt and/or anger.

I think you can live without a lot of things. I don't think you can live without friendship. In fact, researchers at the University of California at Berkeley concluded from a nine-year study that people without friends, spouses, or community ties had a death rate twice as high as those people who had frequent human contact. Friendship, it now appears, can increase and enhance your longevity.

James Allen Sparks, associate professor in the Department of Health and Human Services at the University of Wisconsin at Madison, and a lecturer on the subject of friendship, stated in a magazine article, "It's very easy to procrastinate, but I'm taking more responsibility now for keeping in touch with my special friends. I'm no longer leaving friendship to chance." Nor should you! The only way to have a friend is to be one.

What's Your Friendship Lifestyle?

	YES	NO
Do you have a friend to call when you are sick (to bring groceries, fill a prescription, etc.)?	☐	☐
Is there one friend you can count on day or night (I'm talking about four in the morning when you're sure you're having an appendicitis attack)?	☐	☐
Do you socialize with friends at least twice a week?	☐	☐
Do you have different friends for different occasions (someone to lunch with, someone to play cards with, someone who loves to travel)?	☐	☐
Do you have friends of all ages (at least five years older and five years younger)?	☐	☐
Do you have couples for friends?	☐	☐
Do you have male friends?	☐	☐
Are you open to friendship?	☐	☐
Are *you* a good friend?	☐	☐

There are no right or wrong answers. But the more yeses in your score, the more people in your life. And that's terrific!

Groups as Support

For the past six years I've belonged to a *women's group* to discuss issues related to personal and professional growth. We meet the last Wednesday of every month from six to nine in the evening.

There are twenty members. Because of various schedules, we usually have between twelve to sixteen women in attendance. Their ages range from thirty-five to sixty-four. Some are divorced, some widowed, and some always single. While the group is a mixture of occupations and talents, there are those who are self-employed and those who work in small businesses and in large corporations.

Each month we meet in a different apartment or home. The hostess is responsible for food and drink. (Dinners have included quiche and salad, takeout chicken, ham, pizza, hero sandwiches, stew, cold cuts, and spaghetti and meatballs. The drinks are usually wine, juice, and coffee. Desserts have been cookies, cake, fruit, and cheese.)

Our meeting is structured in the sense that we always begin with a "members' circle." During this time people get a chance to give updates on their lives. We then move into the evening's subject. The end is a go-around of the circle in terms of announcements and requests. ("My friend has a car for sale. Any takers?" "I need an oral surgeon. Anyone have a good one?") The only unbreakable rule is that whatever is discussed *in* the group *stays* in the group.

Once a year we have a retreat where we spend the day (beginning with breakfast and ending at nine in the evening) on various topics that we felt needed further exploration. There's usually lots of laughter, some tears, and an abundance of good feeling.

The group has offered me opportunities for my own growth and development. Listening to how other women handle similar concerns regarding work and love has made me realize that I am not alone with moments of self-doubt. Through some members, I've made professional contacts that have furthered my career. And others in the group have been supportive during periods of physical illness and emotional need. Still others have helped expand my social life.

We turn out in force for each other, be it at a condolence call or at an awards ceremony. And although all of us are not in constant contact, I remain confident that sharing our lives on a regular basis bonds us together.

You can start your own women's group. What are your concerns? Health? Finances? Social life? With what do you need help? What issues need clarification? Begin with a core group of women who know one another. Have each woman bring in someone from outside this nucleus so there is a mix of friends and strangers.

Some topics for consideration might include (1) Relaxation—What Works for Me, (2) Community Action—What to Do, (3) The Best Vacation I Ever Had, (4) How to Work with Your Doctors, (5) Food Co-ops, (6) How to Reduce Stress, (7) The Change in the Status of Women, (8) The Pros and Cons of Marriage, (9) Gossip—Helpful or Hurtful? and (10) Values to Live By.

Group support can also come from *self-help groups* (mutual-aid groups), which are usually leaderless, free of charge, and focused on one particular problem. For instance, there are groups for heart attack survivors (Mended Hearts), parents whose children have died (Compassionate Friends), women with mastectomies (Reach for Recovery), and people with terminal illnesses (Make Today Count). The membership is ongoing, with people dropping in and out according to need or situation.

Self-help groups provide emotional support and practical information for members who are currently dealing with the problem. As one woman reported on her compulsive-spending group, "They know what it's like. They've been in *my* shoes. They understand."

Therapy

We are often blind to our own behavior, to the way we contribute to our problems. We may instead blame others when we ourselves need to accept the responsibility for our circumstances. Sometimes friends can help us with that recognition. Sometimes professional help is needed.

Dr. Mildred Schwartz, a psychologist, views older women as being excellent candidates for psychotherapeutic treatment. She believes that the process can have a liberating effect on the future. This is the opportunity, she believes, to put past problems to rest. "The older woman," she said, "has a more well-defined personality, has had more life experience, and can truly benefit from psychotherapy."

A ninety-six-year-old woman I know has been in psychotherapy for years. "How come?" I wanted to know. "It helps you understand yourself and other people," she replied. "And you're never too old to learn."

Psychotherapy has been referred to as the "talking cure." In a typical forty-five-minute session, you are encouraged to discuss your problems, doubts, and fears. In the safe environment of the office, you can drop your facade and leave your dirty laundry.

A trained, caring, objective professional can help you make connections and interpret feelings. She or he can guide the process whereby you come to terms with who you are and how you behave with others and explore what you would like to become.

To me, asking for help is a sign of strength rather than weakness. It takes a strong person to recognize life is not all he or she wants it to be and then do something about it. Sure, friends can listen to your troubles. But sometimes that's not enough. So when the ache, the anger, or the unhappiness continues, it may be time to get professional help.

Everyone remarked how well Katherine did after Brad's death, especially since it had been so sudden. One minute he was eating breakfast. When she turned from the stove and back to the table, he was dead. "A massive stroke," they said. A widow at sixty-eight, with grown children living out of the state, Katherine carried on her life with grace and dignity. Within ten days she was back to her weekly bridge game, volunteer job, and morning exercise class. She learned how to drive the car she referred to as "Brad's baby," and relied on the manager of her apartment complex for repairs her husband formerly performed.

She was disappointed when both her children canceled their plans to be with her over the Christmas holidays, but she said, "I understood. They had other obligations."

After New Year's, Katherine began to fall apart. She found herself unable to get out of bed in the morning. Instead of getting up with the alarm, she'd turn it off and go back to sleep. She made it to her exercise class three mornings out of five; then it was down to two, and a short while later, she simply stopped making the effort.

She pleaded sickness to her bridge partners and to her supervisor at the adult education center where she volunteered her time.

Although the feeling of fatigue continued throughout the day, Katherine began to find herself unable to sleep at night. She tried to read but was unable to concentrate. Nothing held her interest.

When Amy, fifty-six, moved to Arizona because of her health, she saw it as a great adventure. After five months of job hunting, she settled into the only position she could find—one for which she was overqualified.

At the end of ten months, her health had not improved, she'd made no close friends, and she'd begun to have frequent arguments at work.

During a telephone conversation with a friend from her hometown, she began to cry, and hung up in the middle of a sentence. She described her feelings simply: "Once I started, I was afraid I'd never stop." But she did stop, and she did calm down with the help of tranquilizers prescribed by a doctor for back pain.

She began to move through her days in a fog. Her work—what she completed—was below standard. She had almost no appetite and dropped nine pounds from her already slender frame.

———————

Berda's son had been in trouble all his life, yet she continued to "rescue" him. An out-of-work alcoholic, he lived in a nearby rooming house.

Struggling to make ends meet, Berda, fifty-five, a divorcée for over a decade, worked two jobs. Every time she managed to save, to get a little ahead, her son would make another demand. And once again, true to pattern, she would bail him out.

During a recent three-month period, her son had taken to dropping in at all hours of the day and night. If Berda was out, she'd return to find her apartment littered with beer cans and dirty dishes. Pieces of costume jewelry began to disappear and even some of her appliances. When she confronted her son, he became verbally abusive and threatening.

Formerly outgoing, she became silent and with-drawn—scared of her own shadow, fearful of her son's rage. Ashamed and wary of her son's erratic behavior, she stopped socializing with friends and kept more and more to herself.

———————

In all three cases, the women's day-to-day function-ing became impaired. All received professional help, though the ways and means to aid differed.

One of Katherine's bridge partners, also a widow, recommended a psychologist at an analytic institute.

Amy's boss, disturbed by her job performance and apparent disintegration, suggested a psychiatrist.

And Berda, tired of being victimized, began to see a social worker at a neighborhood mental health clinic.

You should consider professional help if a majority of the following statements can apply to you.

☐ I'm dissatisfied with my behavior and feelings.

- ☐ I'm experiencing a problem that causes unusual distress.
- ☐ I frequently feel anxious, yet there appears to be no discernible cause.
- ☐ I'm overly dependent on pills, alcohol, or food.
- ☐ I no longer find pleasure in anything I do.
- ☐ I frequently feel depressed and unhappy.
- ☐ I find myself crying for no apparent reason.
- ☐ I have numerous physical symptoms for which there are no medical solutions.
- ☐ I've noticed a change in my personal habits that I feel powerless to overcome.
- ☐ I feel constantly angry and provoke arguments with family and friends.

Whom should you see? The *social worker* has attended graduate school for a specialized two-year program that grants an MSW (Master of Social Work) degree. Social workers are trained to help individuals, couples, and families.

The graduate training for a clinical *psychologist* involves academic work and practical experience. On completion of from four to five years of study, the psychologist is granted a Ph.D. degree.

The *psychiatrist* is a physician who has completed a residency in psychiatry. He or she holds an M.D. degree and is able to prescribe drugs.

The *pastoral counselor* is a member of the clergy who usually has a psychology or social work background. Check for certification by the American Association of Pastoral Counselors.

Try to remember that the alleviation of problems and feelings of distress usually doesn't happen overnight or after one therapy session. Treatment can last from weeks to years, depending on the nature of your problem.

Fees are usually set according to your income and according to where you are seen by the professional—in a private practice or in a clinic setting.

Although you make a commitment to a therapist or counselor, *you* are the one who has to do the work, and *you* are, ultimately, the only one who can effect a change.

You have the *right* to obtain the best possible professional treatment. If your therapist suggests meetings outside the office, makes direct sexual advances, appears to be using alcohol or drugs, and/or breaks the principle of confidentiality without your consent, *you must* terminate your relationship. The preceding indications are examples of unethical conduct and should not be tolerated.

To find professional help, you can contact any of the following sources.

□ your family doctor
□ the local mental health association
□ the National Organization for Women
□ an analytic training institute
□ the psychiatry department of your local hospital
□ someone you know who has successfully undergone treatment

Before you decide, obtain answers to these questions.

□ What about training and credentials? What was the course of study? What degree was granted? Has the professional had postgraduate training?
□ How long has the professional been in practice? Has the person worked with other people with problems similar to yours?
□ What is the policy regarding canceled sessions and vacation periods?
□ Can the professional be reached by telephone in an emergency?
□ Is the professional affiliated with a hospital, medical doctor, or psychiatrist in case medication is needed?
□ If psychological treatment is covered by your health insurance policy, is the practitioner licensed to sign your insurance forms?
□ And perhaps the most important criterion for selection—are you *comfortable* with the person? Do you

feel supported? Do you feel safe? Is he or she some-one you can trust? someone you can like? (If not, leave!)

Interview at least three professionals before you make your decision. (If you are currently in treatment, you may want to evaluate your growth and rate of change periodically. If at any time the results of this examination prove unsatisfactory, you may want or need to change therapists.)

Another type of treatment, possibly less expensive, is *group therapy*. This form of therapy offers the indi-vidual many things. It can serve as a new family in which other members remind you of certain relatives. The way you related to them in the past can now be reworked so your problems in interactions are not hampered in the present. Or your group may be com-posed of people with whom you would never want to associate. Then you'd need, and would learn, to ques-tion your judgments, perceptions, and viewpoints about people different from you.

In group therapy you can try on new roles and watch how your behavior affects others. You can clar-ify your own thoughts by listening to how other members deal with their problems. And you can gain a new sense of self-esteem as you participate in the give-and-take of group process.

Group therapy is run by a qualified leader. The sessions are confidential, with members encouraged not to meet or discuss the material outside of the group.

Lucille Beards is seventy-five and has parlayed her role of grandmother into a thriving business. The sky-blue brochure for Grandma Lends a Listening Ear states in part, "When you need someone to talk to who is successful in relationships, Grandma is ready to help by listening ... ready to help with understanding, warmth and caring." Lucille has two children and three grandchildren. She was divorced when she was fifty-five.

"I feel as if I spent my life doing volunteer work. I was a nurse's aide. Then I spent twenty years creating and running a fine arts center for emotionally disturbed teenagers. I had people teach classes in art, music, and dance. On and off during those years I ran a thrift shop to get the money to support the center.

"I never worked for a salary till I was seventy. A friend asked if I wanted to be the assistant manager of a thrift shop he was running. Since my divorce, my lifestyle has changed. My income was less than my expenses. Can you imagine, at seventy I became a breadwinner! But that's my daytime job.

"One night I was in my bedroom, and I was thinking about myself. What was I qualified for? What did I really love? Those are two questions anyone at any age must ask. And I remember I went like that [snapped her fingers] and said, 'I've got it: Grandma Lends a Listening Ear.'

"I feel people need to ventilate; they need someone to talk to. A problem just magnifies itself; it becomes a big burden, a giant. And if you face it, if you call upon your own common sense, all the things that normally are there—unless the panic button's pushed—you can handle pretty much everything.

"There are so few grandmas who are really actively up-to-date and open and free. That's something I felt I had. I felt I was in touch with the needs of young people.

"I asked myself how I was going to do it. Where would I reach the people? I put the brochure together myself. My thought was to approach the doctors who are very busy, the lawyers who are busy, the dentists—wherever I could get referrals. So I started with the doctors, dentists, and lawyers I knew and wrote them a little letter by hand.

"I was aiming for anyone of any age who had difficulty handling problems, crises, or decisions. I think the very first person recommended to me was getting a divorce; he was in his forties. Then there was a girl who was having difficulty with jobs; she could never stay more than seven or eight months. I'm equipped to be a caring, listening sounding board. People come to my home in the evenings and on weekends. My grandson, who is in his twenties, said, 'Just keep it homey and chatty,' and I thought that was so marvelous because, 'homey and chatty,' we don't hear that anymore. We've lost that in the shuffle.

"If I were to give advice to other grandmothers on dealing with their grandchildren, I'd say, 'Watch and listen as if you're in a theater.' You're not there to tell them all about yourself. If you listen to music, you can either hear music or listen to it. And most people want to be heard. Now, my advice is that the grand-mothers look first to themselves—the grandmother must first look into herself and then count on her real built-in love. Nobody at any age wants to be greeted with 'You should have,' 'You could have,' 'You don't do.' So, really, there's very little difference between grandmothers' relating to grandchildren and grand-mothers relating to neighbors. And just because you're a relative, that doesn't give you the right to direct them.

"I don't think of the calendar. I don't feel any different than when I was thirty. And time, as you get older, is more and more exciting. I work; I keep up my three-room apartment; I control my life. But the good part comes when you can control the stress. For instance, I got a call from my former husband about financial things. I could feel myself get sort of flustered—I could feel the blood pressure—and I said, 'Now, just a minute. You'll be able to handle whatever comes from this conversation.' So we fin-ished the conversation, and I still felt this flutter. It was 9:30 P.M., so I said, 'Now, just get up and go inside and read.' I put other thoughts inside my mind. Our brains are like computers. And whatever you think, that's what you're going to hear—that's the beeper.

And I let a day or two go by, and I called him on the phone and said, 'Now, is this what you really mean and blah, blah, blah.' And I had absolute control of myself.

"I don't allow anyone—not the grandchildren, not my own children—to pull the rug from under my feet. I have the privilege of controlling myself. You cannot control another person. But you can control your language, your feelings. You can control your actions. You can control your thinking. As soon as you say, 'But I,' you're allowing a negative thought to come into that mental computer. Negative thoughts will come, but don't let them take over. Once I had a stack of bills—everybody has financial problems *these* days—and I said, 'Great, that's prosperity. If I didn't have bills, I wouldn't have credit.' And I put my hand on the bills and said, 'You are all going to be paid.' But at that moment I couldn't pay the telephone company the full amount, so I wrote out a check for whatever I could give them at the time. And I felt free.

"In terms of health, I have the smallest size aspirin in the house in case somebody comes with a headache. I attribute my really good health to—I know some people would say genes, but it's not that—developing control over stress. If you make a fist, and this is a good test, you can see the whole arm tighten. It goes through the neck; the whole body becomes tense. I remember I fell down a flight of stairs and wound up in an ambulance. I had pins and needles in the extremities, the ends of the fingers, so I felt I'd broken my neck. In the ambulance I said, 'Now, just concentrate on breathing. In spite of the pain, breathe.' I came through. I had to wear a collar. I had no aftereffects whatsoever. If the body is not relaxed, you'll get ulcers and all kinds of things. I don't think my diet is anything special. I eat whatever I want. I did a great deal of dancing in my life. So very often when I walk, I'll say, 'Now, walk the way you did when you used to dance.' I feel you don't need to go to a gymnasium to exercise. You can do it right where you are.

"If I like someone, I go all out, no holds barred. I have no designs on anyone else. I have no control over anyone else. I didn't marry again, but I've had men in my life at different periods. Any man I ever went with, I can still pick up the phone and see again. They don't leave.

"In actuality, we are individuals, and we are alone. It's wonderful to be alone—it's a luxury. It's not 'I'm a discard' or 'I'm not worthy' or anything else. We're all individuals; nobody can feel your joy, and nobody can feel your pain. But where you're not alone is if you give in the simplest way—you share. There's no difference between giving and taking, as I see it, because a person who gives is receiving something far more than if you're giving someone a gift. You're receiving the joy of sharing.

"Life doesn't owe me. I owe everything to life."

For More Information

Organizations

The National Self-Help Clearinghouse (Graduate School and University Center/CUNY, 33 West 42nd Street, Room 1227, New York, NY 10036) publishes a free newsletter about self-help groups around the country. They are also able to put you in touch with a group in your area.

Or request the free fact sheet, "Mutual Help Groups" (540L) from the Consumer Information Center, Pueblo, CO 81009.

Two groups able to provide information related to the "sandwich generation" are Children of Aging Parents, 2761 Trenton Road, Levittown, PA 19056, and the National Support Center for Families of the Aging, PO Box 245, Swarthmore, PA 19081.

The General Federation of Women's Clubs, 1734 N Street, NW, Washington, DC 20036, has programs dealing with aging parents in all Junior Division clubs.

You can write for information regarding the treatment of phobias to the American Psychiatric Association, 1700 Eighteenth Street, NW, Washington, DC 20009, and to the American Psychological Association, 1200 Seventeenth Street, NW, Washington, DC 20036.

Books

Budman, Simon. *Forms of Brief Therapy.* New York: Guilford Press, 1981.

Denniston, Denise, and Peter McWilliams. *The TM Book: How to Enjoy the Rest of Your Life.* Los Angeles: Price, Stern, Sloan Pubs., 1975.

Ehrenberg, Otto, and Miriam Ehrenberg. *The Psychotherapy Maze: A Consumer's Guide to the Ins and Outs of Therapy.* New York: Holt, Rinehart & Winston, 1979.

Herink, Richie, ed. *The Psychotherapy Handbook.* New York: New American Library, 1980.

Muktananda, Swami. *Meditate.* Albany, N.Y.: State Univ. of New York Press, 1980.

Sutherland, E. Ann, and Amit Zalman. With Andrew Weiner. *Phobia Free: How to Fight Your Fears.* New York: Harcourt Brace Jovanovich, 1977.

Viscott, David, M.D. *The Viscott Method: A Revolutionary Program for Self-Analysis and Self-Understanding.* Boston: Houghton Mifflin Co., 1984.

6

Social Life

No one can make you feel inferior without your consent.

—Eleanor Roosevelt

It is hard being a social single. It is even harder when you have always thought of yourself as part of a couple. There is a sense of security in knowing you arrive and leave with that certain someone. There is a feeling of comfort in entering a strange situation when you've got a significant other at your side. For those of you who are newly single, I've got news. You're an acceptable person *without* a partner. And to those always single, yes, I agree, it's tough entering a room where you don't know anyone. Newly or always single, social lives go on, and so will yours.

Social Tasks

To make things easier in new situations, get some information before you go. What will the women be wearing? How large will the gathering be? Will there only be couples, or will there be a mix of people? Do you know anyone else who is invited? Will you be able to get a lift home?

Give yourself some social tasks. Tell yourself, I won't leave this party until (1) I've talked to six people,

(2) I've taken someone's phone number, (3) I've made a lunch date, and (4) I've flirted with the most attractive man present.

You don't have to stay anywhere until the bitter end. Leave when you've had enough, but do give yourself a chance. In the beginning, try to stay at least an hour. So you feel awkward. That's okay. You won't die. Take your mind off yourself. Observe the other women. Talk to someone standing alone. Perhaps that person is also feeling unsure, shy, tentative. Go out of your way to make someone else feel comfortable. You might join a small group of people who are talking and introduce yourself or simply make a comment appropriate to the discussion. It's worth a try.

With couples, there's usually a period of estrangement while people sort out their feelings as to your single state. "I remember having dinner with two couples we'd known for years. It was terrible. Every time I brought up Milt's name, they changed the subject or told me not to get upset. *I* wasn't upset. Milt was a fine man, a loving husband, a good friend. To pretend he wasn't dead, or that he never existed, negated him and me." (Lee, sixty.)

And Pearl, fifty-five, recounted her experience as a divorcée: "I think right after the divorce, our friends didn't know how to deal with me. Harry just walked out one morning and by evening was living five blocks away with his dental hygienist. I think all around there was a great feeling of embarrassment. I waited it out and learned who were my true friends."

How can you socialize with couples? Take them out to dinner. Call the restaurant in advance and arrange for the maître d' or the person serving your table to present *you* with the check. If couples continually take you out, reciprocate. Have them over for drinks before or for dessert after. Remember, these are people whom you like and enjoy. Be yourself.

Taking good care of your social life means taking good care of yourself during the lonely times. Plan,

plan, plan. Where can you meet new people? Have you networked? Do people know you're looking for a bridge game? a tennis partner? a date? People can't read your mind. Have you been open about your needs? If you are out there—if you are participating in life by taking courses, doing volunteer work, being involved with political action, or building hobbies— you are bound to meet people. And some of those people will undoubtedly become friends.

When was the last time you went to any of these:

an art show	the library
the ballet	a movie
the circus	a museum
a concert	the opera
a discussion group	a play
a fashion show	a poetry reading
a lecture	the zoo

So, if not *now*, when? Choose three places to visit during the next month. Go by yourself or invite a friend to go with you.

"Just because I'm single, I refuse to deny myself the social activities I loved when I was part of a couple. The opera and the ballet are still special to me. Sometimes I have to force myself to get there because I'm self-conscious going alone. Then I think of the music or the dancing, and I'm out the door." (Suzanne, fifty-nine.)

"When I get to the theater alone, I go early. I make it a point to get seated and scout the audience for other singles. At intermission I try to engage someone in conversation. After the play I always try to comment to someone about the content or performance. I've found people are eager to share their opinions. If the conversation is interesting, I might suggest continuing it over coffee at a nearby restaurant. I've made a number of new friends this way." (Lucy, sixty-two.)

To nurture friendships, to enlarge your support system, and to build your social life, you'll need to entertain. Having people in or taking them out deepens a relationship and gives you a chance to increase your social options. Generally, the more you entertain, the more people will reciprocate with invitations of their own, and so it goes. (Think of throwing a pebble into a lake and watching the expanding circles. Invitations can have that same effect.)

How Other Women Entertain

☐ "I feel that if there's no occasion, you should make one. I'm ready to celebrate anything at the drop of a hat. I had six people in for dinner last week because a sixty-four-year-old friend passed her driver's test."

☐ "I take people out to dinner. I don't have to fuss or prepare or get stuck with the dishes."

☐ "Brunch is my answer. Some good breads, a few interesting chunks of cheese, pots of coffee, and a killer dessert make even the sleepyheads wake up."

☐ "I have two large cocktail parties a year, one in the fall and one in the spring. It gives me a chance to pay back some of the social invitations I've received. I go all-out—fancy dress, a college student as bartender, and loads of fresh flowers."

☐ "I'm known for my spaghetti sauce and usually have a spaghetti dinner the last Friday of the month. It's very casual, very informal. I have a mixed group of people, whomever I ran into or met that month."

☐ "I have lots of dinner parties. I'm not sitting back waiting for a good time. I go and create a good time for myself and others."

☐ "I like to throw people from different parts of my life together, for example, some people from the hospital where I volunteer, my hairdresser, the librarian, some bridge partners, and my accountant. What a mix!"

☐ "Potluck dinners, where each person brings a family-sized portion of anything, work for me. After we eat, I like to have some activity—play readings, charades, a game of bingo."

☐ "Entertaining friends becomes very important when you're single. I try to have numerous small dinners during the year. I always serve ethnic food—Jamaican, Hungarian, Korean—because then I learn something new in the process. I have a collection of unusual ethnic cookbooks."

Meeting Men

If you're interested, where and how do you meet men? The where I sometimes think is easier than the how. If you're out in the world and breathing, there are men all around you. Think of last week and all the men in your proximity: that man in the bank line, the one pushing a cart in the market, the person at the community center, the cousin visiting a next-door neighbor. You've seen them. So they're not Cary Grant or Robert Redford. (How many men are?) We're not playing instant "Dating Game." I'm talking men as friends, to start. And if you don't open your mouth and say, "Hello," "My, this line is long," "Do you come here often?" "I'd like to meet your cousin," they'll remain strangers, and you can bemoan the fact that you never meet any new men.

The reality is that people want to meet other people. New methods constantly are being promoted. Some are valid, and some are not. If you decide to try any of them, make sure you do your homework and investigate the claims and contracts.

Video-dating takes the "blind" out of blind dates. You make a videotape (it's painless) in which you discuss your interests, hobbies, and goals. Then you look and listen to tapes made by men. You choose the men that interest you. Those men get called to look at your tape, and if one likes what he sees, it's a match. It also works the other way around. There must be mutual consent before phone numbers are exchanged.

Introduction services are matchmakers at work. You're interviewed, and a profile is drawn up. From the men on file, the interviewer selects someone compatible. Phone numbers are given out. The rest is up to you.

Newest on the scene are *personal ads*. You can answer or place one. I think you have more control when you write the ad and have all those letters to choose from. For instance:

60ish blue-eyed woman, kind, affectionate, athletic, theater-goer seeks same for friendship and possible romance.
Photo, phone # appreciated. Box 1804

Petite widow, 54, enjoys gourmet cooking, golf, reading, laughter, and special man, 50–65.
Bio/photo/phone. Box 1805

Initials are sometimes used in the body of the ad: *Bi*, bisexual; *Bl*, black; *C*, Christian; *D*, divorced; *F*, female; *G*, gay; *J*, Jewish; *M*, married or male, depending on where it's placed—as adjective, married, as noun, male; *S*, single; *WASP*, white Anglo-Saxon Protestant; *W*, white. If you choose to meet someone from an ad, *always* pick a public place for the first date.

The services described are costly. Yet people do meet (or they'd be out of business), friendships are formed, and marriages are made.

You can also meet men at organized activities for *singles only*. These may include weekends at a hotel, dinner parties held at different restaurants, athletic events, concert socials, bus tours, rap groups, and lectures. Consult your newspaper, community center, and houses of worship for listings.

"But, Mom . . ." Some older women who may be ready to lead active social and sexual lives may be forced into loneliness by their children's censure. An adult child who says to his widowed mother, "What would Father think?" creates guilt where none should be. Psychoanalyst Dr. Fred Lipschitz believes sons feel very proprietary about their mothers' relationships, whereas daughters tend to be more accepting. Women need to believe they have "a right to their own life, to companionship, to physical satisfaction. And," continued Dr. Lipschitz, "this should be presented to the children in a positive light. For example, 'I'm happy that I met someone I like to play golf with. I have a right to enjoy this man and his companionship.'"

Yet, not every single woman wants a man in her life. Some have discovered themselves. And in the process they have become independent and quite content to go it alone. Clara, fifty-nine, said, "I don't want to feed medicine to some old man in my twilight years. Why should I be bothered by someone who may become ill at this stage of my life? I'm okay with myself—with my part-time job, cards, hobbies, and kids."

Being a Grandmother

Social life for some means being a grandparent. Abigail, seventy-four, fairly glowed. "I love being a grandmother. I can spoil them, spoil them some more, and then send them home when I'm tired. I don't criticize. I give love, support, affection. I'm in their corner no matter what. They live down the block, and I see them on a daily basis."

Barbara, fifty-eight, felt somewhat different. "I love my grandchildren—but at a distance. I raised three kids by myself. I'm tired. When I socialize, I want it to be with people who are walking, not crawling. Toddlerhood was never my favorite period. I don't mean to sound harsh, but I resent being unpaid labor. I'm available for emergencies and for visits that have been mutually arranged. I'm not available to be taken advantage of."

Being a grandmother means passing on history. You can give your children's children a feeling for another time—the time when you grew up. You can also pass along tradition and a sense of family. To the child experiencing rough moments with his or her parents, you can be the buffer and mediator, the one to give perspective. And you can share with your grandchild what his or her parent was like growing up.

If you live too far to visit, there's the mail and the telephone. Stay in touch. Explain your life. Dispel the notion of the picture books—you know, the ones with grandma rocking away her days on the front porch.

A word of caution: You can overdo anything. Use, don't abuse, the role of grandmother. Aside from that role, you're still an active single woman. Don't rely on your children or grandchildren to fill the holes in your life.

Eating Alone

Elaine, sixty-one, an active grandmother of three, felt her biggest social problem was eating alone. "I manage to fill my time creatively. I feel I'm very involved with life. I have friends, and yet some evenings I get so damn tired of having dinner with Dan Rather." Hold on a minute. You've got options.

Over the years, I've run many groups for single women. One assignment that always brings groans is to eat out alone—first at a coffee shop, then at a restaurant with tablecloths and napkins. Women pass the coffee shop test with flying colors. But, oh, the restaurant assignment! What is it about a tablecloth and napkin and being alone that so intimidates us as women? Here's how some women voiced their concerns.

"Everyone will look at me." And what if they do? They're probably wishing they had the nerve to eat alone. Or maybe they're admiring your hair or outfit. What's bad about that?

"I've never done it." Well, there are probably lots of things you've never done. It doesn't mean you can't begin, right now.

"I can prepare it myself." Sure you can, but the idea is to have someone do it for you. Let someone else cook, serve, and clean up. This is supposed to be a treat, not hard labor.

"I never know what to tip." You can learn. Talk to friends. See how they handle it. In general you usually tip 15 percent of the bill *before the tax*. You tip 20 percent if the service has been exceptional or you want to be generous.

"I'd be uncomfortable." Maybe you would. But no one ever died from discomfort. New things are scary. They become less so as you try them out.

"I'd rather eat with a friend." Yes, it's nice eating out with a friend. But let's say you have plans. You're looking forward to dinner, and then your friend cancels because of illness. Why should you miss out on a pleasant experience? Get dressed and go!

How Other Women Handle Eating Alone in a Restaurant

- "I try to go to a restaurant at off-peak hours—before 6:00 or after 7:30."
- "I think of something that needs resolution or concentrate on pleasant memories. I *do not* focus on being alone."
- "I go where I'm known to the management."
- "Eating in places with music seems to make it easier for me."
- "I choose to have my main meal out in the middle of the day and a light one at home in the evening."
- "I think of eating out as a celebration; I'm being served, and someone else is doing the dishes!"
- "I enjoy eating out because I'm a blatant, unobtrusive eavesdropper."
- "I tell myself that eating out is a special occasion and I deserve the best."
- "I choose restaurants that are small and cozy."
- "Bringing along some reading material helps me feel more secure and less conspicuous."

□ "I call ahead and make a reservation. This way they know what they're getting, and I don't feel unexpected."

Eating alone in a restaurant doesn't make you a second-class citizen. You have the right not to be seated in oblivion. You have the right to have cold food cold and hot food hot. You have the right to send back food. You have the right to fast, courteous service that is not rushed. And, most important, you have the right to *enjoy* eating alone.

If any of these rights are denied, it's up to *you* to take action. Use a chain of command. First, complain to the waiter. ("I'd rather sit over there." "This is not hot. I'd like another serving." "This doesn't taste right. I'd like to order something else." "I feel as if you're rushing me.") If you aren't satisfied, ask to speak to the manager.

If you go alone, it doesn't mean you have to dine that way. Numerous restaurants across the country are inaugurating tables for single people (the Captain's Table). You enter alone but are seated with other singles. It's an interesting way to make new friends.

Or, why not talk to that single man or woman waiting to be seated? Perhaps join forces? And, if you're seated next to another single diner, why not strike up a conversation? The opportunities are there. You just have to take them.

And if you are eating at home? You can eat alone and be human. You don't *have to* stand up and gobble your food over the sink. You don't *have to* eat in your nightgown and robe. You don't *have to* dine on potato chips and packaged cupcakes.

How Other Women Handle Eating Alone at Home

□ "When I eat at home, my constant companion is the stereo."
□ "I prepare a batch of food in advance and then freeze it in meal-sized portions."

□ "An at-home dinner treat is to order in Chinese food and eat in bed, propped up by pillows, and watching the television."

□ "A neighbor and I cook for each other once a week. We each make enough of something for two large servings; then we exchange. Sometimes I'll eat her dinner that night, or I may freeze it for later in the week."

□ "I put on my favorite symphony, use my best china, and have wine with dinner."

□ "Whether it's steak or tuna fish salad, I always dine by candlelight."

My mother used to tell me when I was growing up, "You have one stomach. Treat it well." I would now add, "And treat your mealtimes as special occasions." Whether you're in a restaurant or your home, relax and enjoy!

For More Information

Books

Buscaglia, Leo. *Loving Each Other*. Thorofare, N.J.: Slack, 1984.

Davis, Lynn. *The Lynn Davis Guide to Personal Ads*. New York: Purcell Productions, 1983.

Friedman, James T. *The Divorce Handbook*. New York: Random House, 1982.

Sills, Judith. *How to Stop Looking for Someone Perfect and Find Someone to Love*. New York: St. Martin's Press, 1984.

Sternberg, Patricia. *Be My Friend: The Art of Good Relationships*. Philadelphia, PA: Westminster Press, 1983.

Weber, Eric. *The Divorced Woman's Guide to Meeting New Men*. New York: William Morrow & Co., 1984.

7

Holidays

I refuse to deal
With another New Year's Eve party.
A programmed evening
With forced gaiety, artificial laughter
And deliberate drunkenness.
Next year I will stay home
By myself
And welcome in the New Year
Alone and at peace.

—Jane Seskin

I remember giving an interview to a local paper on how to survive the holidays—on how to cope with seasonal depression. I was sparkly, informed, and logical. I was in control. And then, three days later, there I was, walking down the street past the gaily decorated stores, through the crowds of bustling shoppers, with tears running down my cheeks. And I learned.

I learned that sometimes your head and heart may not be in sync. I learned that my feelings were close to the surface, which meant I was in touch with my sadness and the longings from the past. The tears didn't make me melt. Sure, I felt self-conscious (I don't usually walk along the streets sobbing), but that was transitory. I knew that in the evening I'd be with people I liked. There would be good food, good talk, and good feeling. I had learned to take care of myself, and you can too.

Romanticizing the Past

The holidays prompt us to think about our lives—about our families, about ties that have been lost, about relationships that have been broken, and about desires that have not been fulfilled.

Holidays mean nostalgia. They are a way of marking time. As I've listened over the years to women reflect on the reminders of the past, I'm struck by how often those periods are romanticized. Theirs was the plumpest turkey, the tallest tree, the happiest guests. There were descriptions of scenes to rival a Norman Rockwell painting. Were they accurate, or were they idealizations?

If they were accurate, by all means acknowledge the good memories. If they were good, why wipe them out of your mind? Recall those special moments with tenderness and then let them go. The past is just that—past. Now, *get on with your future!*

Expecting Too Much

The trouble with holidays is that we expect so much from them. (This feeling is not restricted to single people.) *If* you get that certain present, *if* you're invited to that special party, *if* so-and-so calls—well, everything will be better. But will it, or do we just wish it to be so and then inevitably become disappointed when the fantasy bubble bursts?

I think the first thing you need to do is be realistic. What were the holidays really like for you? Make a list. Write down all the good things you associate with those special times of the year. Now, on another sheet of paper, list all the difficult things, all the problem areas you can remember. (Did you cook for days? invite people you didn't want? Were you too tired to enjoy yourself?) Okay. Now you're done, finished with those difficult things. Crumple up that list and throw it away. You no longer have to be bothered with things you don't want to do. Keep the other list and incorporate the good things into your single life.

Holidays, the big ones that occur during the winter months (Thanksgiving, Christmas, New Year's), may also be depression-inducing just *because* of the season. It's cold and dark outside. It feels gloomy. Yet everyone is *supposed* to be happy. Isn't that the message from the media? from the world?

The Save-a-Life League, a nationwide suicide prevention group, puts on extra staff during the month of December.

The New York City Medical Examiner's office says that the number of suicides rises by about one-third around holiday times, going from between twenty and twenty-five weekly to between thirty and forty.

And according to Manhattan psychoanalyst Dolores Nicoll, depression is "fairly common" during this time. "It's either you had something, and you feel the loss, or you never had it, and you wonder what's wrong with you." Feeling deprived or like a victim are recurring themes with the single women she sees. "But," Ms. Nicoll suggests, "you are not helpless. You *can* motivate yourself."

I would go one step further and add this: You *can* be self-protective. You don't have to get "caught up" with the season. You don't have to go to a party, get drunk, or be happy. You don't have to be pressured to join in organized fun, renew old relationships, or brave the mob-filled department stores. You don't have to outspend or out-gift friends or relatives. You don't have to go off your diet to be sociable. Accept yourself as you are. *It's no disgrace to feel blue.* But if you find you are crying a lot, continuously overeating, having temper tantrums, depending on drugs, depending on alcohol, or not getting out of bed in the morning, and these symptoms last for more than ten days, seek help. (See pages 91–101 on where to find emotional support.)

Planning Ahead

What's the date today? What's the next holiday on the calendar? Get a pencil and a piece of paper. List three things you might plan to do. Tape the list to your mirror or refrigerator door. Between now and the coming holiday clarify your program.

I can recall one New Year's Eve when I vowed I wouldn't go to a party populated by strangers. And my close friends were all out of town. One week before "the night" I thought about what I'd like to do, what would make me happy with myself, and then set about actualizing my plans. I bought two paperbacks I'd been anxious to read but hadn't yet had time for. A lover of starch (but a constant dieter), I spent a day making homemade spaghetti sauce to go over my homemade pasta, purchased a fabulous loaf of bread and two slices of cheesecake at a gourmet shop near my home, and splurged on a good bottle of wine.

Cozily nestled in my bed, I read and ate and watched TV. It was one of the nicest holiday evenings I've had.

It was nice because I indulged myself, because I'd planned how I would spend my time and wasn't caught unprepared, because I found that it was all right to be quiet as the rest of the world played midnight madness, and because *being alone didn't have to mean being lonely.*

How to Prevent Holiday Blues

□ Don't be afraid to admit you have no plans. If people *assume* you're busy, they won't extend an invitation.

□ If no one asks you, ask them! Call a friend or an acquaintance. Suggest a movie and/or dinner out.

□ Call a number of people for a potluck dessert party. Have each person *you* call, call one of *his or her* friends. You'll wind up meeting a whole new group of people and have a major taste experience to boot.

- Invite your neighbors (what better way to start building a support system?) in for eggnog and cookies.
- Plan ahead. I'm talking a couple of weeks, not the day before. Ask around. Be a detective. Who's doing what? Where? Something happening at your church? job? community center?
- Buy a puzzle with at least five hundred pieces. Invite some people over to help you put it together.
- This might be your chance to take advantage of a suddenly empty city or town. See the movie that usually has long lines. Go to the play, show, or event previously sold out. Attend the concert you never had time for but wanted to hear. Give yourself an out-of-the-house treat.
- Take a trip. Go to a new city or state or go out of the country. Join a tour; see the sights; make new friends. This requires some good planning, so start thinking now where you'd like to spend the next holiday.
- Cry. Yes, you read that right. Give into the sadness, the loneliness, the old associations. Okay, time's up. Now get on with your plans.
- *You* make the decision. *Choose* to enjoy yourself.

How Other Women Handle the Holidays

- "I don't allow myself to be depressed. I am optimistic and carry my happiness with me."
- "I keep a distance from people who are 'downers.'"
- "I shut the blinds, pull up the covers, and sleep."
- "I go to movie revival houses because the shows are better on holidays."
- "I try to keep in mind that the holidays will pass, just as a rainy day will end."
- "One year at Christmas when I'd made no plans, I posted a sign in my lobby and asked everyone to come to my apartment with a dish and an inexpensive grab bag present. It was a grand party!"

□ "I think of the holiday as being one of the regular, ordinary days and do small things that need to be taken care of but which I never seem to have time for."

□ "I get in my car and drive with no destination in mind. I love to cruise through new neighborhoods admiring the lights and decorations."

□ "I'm not religious, but I do have a tree and a trimming party on Christmas Eve. I ask my friends to bring an object or favorite greeting card to hang."

□ "I call a friend at 11:45 on New Year's Eve. We talk our way through the 'witching hour.'"

□ "I spend the holidays making things—candles, preserves, pot holders, scarves—for the pharmacist, cleaner, beautician, mailman. I make it a point to deliver them after Christmas."

□ "I invite people over Christmas Day for a very low-keyed, informal games party. I set up tables with Scrabble, cards, dominoes, Monopoly, checkers, and backgammon. There are inexpensive gifts for the winners and gag prizes for the losers. Everyone goes home with something."

□ "Since I love to sing, I make note of all the holiday choral groups that are looking for volunteers— they're usually listed in the papers. Sometimes I have to force myself to get there, but I *do* get there and always wind up enjoying the camaraderie and spirit."

□ "I've had a large potluck supper the second week in January for the past five years. It's become a tradition. People are too frazzled during the holidays to enjoy anything or anyone. If they've been away, this gives them another opportunity to share the New Year holiday with friends. My time is spent planning, decorating the house, and preparing food. I have a goal to get me happily and busily through what had formerly been a low-energy, lonely time."

☐ "I cajole a friend into exercising with me. We take a long walk and go bowling, ice skating, or swimming at the local Y. Sure, we feel tired. But we also feel virtuous and healthy. And we've had fun!"

☐ "I have six to ten people in for apple cider or mulled wine. I ask each person to bring a favorite record album. We talk and drink and listen to music. It's cozy and comfortable."

Sharing with Others

One of the best ways to spend a holiday is to share with others. Give someone the gift of *you*.

☐ Call the Salvation Army, a local church, the closest foster care agency, or a neighborhood senior citizens center and ask for the name of a needy family. Put together a holiday gift package and deliver it.

☐ Contact a local college or foreign-student center. Invite some students to dinner.

☐ Make a pancake breakfast for the neighborhood children on New Year's Day. Their parents will thank you for the year.

☐ Volunteer your time for the day to a hospital or nursing home.

☐ Bake up a storm! Try new recipes. Bake cookies, cakes, pies, breads, and/or muffins. Then give them all away.

☐ Write catch-up letters to all the people you've neglected during the year.

When you give to others, you give to yourself.

Holidays will only become a problem if you make them so. YOU have the power to plan your time, to take care of yourself, to create your very own special kind of day. *Do it!*

8

Your Financial Self

Not what you possess but what you do with what you have, determines your true worth.

—Thomas Carlyle

Woman A: "I don't have a head for figures." Woman B: "I never got past tenth-grade math." Woman C: "I turn over everything to my son." Do any of these women sound like you?

We have for too long relied on others for making our financial decisions. There may have been a father, then a husband, then a lawyer. While I'm not knocking any of these people in terms of advice giving (we may need their expertise), I *am* concerned about women who take no part in these decisions. The getting, keeping, building, and maintaining of a sound economic base must be addressed by each of us, in our own individual way.

Taking Responsibility

As a single woman, working or retired, you are responsible for your life. To survive with any degree of comfort takes money and wise planning. If you do decide to turn over your financial responsibilities, at least be aware of how your money will be spent.

It would be wonderful if someone left you an inheritance or if you unexpectedly won a contest. Those windfalls, unfortunately, can't be guaranteed. And while the fantasy is delicious, the fact is *you* are going to have to provide for *your* self.

When I asked a group of women where they went for financial advice, I was surprised by the large number who turn to a member of their family. While some relatives may be eminently qualified, I continue to believe that if you want advice, you learn what you need to know yourself and, if necessary, you consult a professional (not a younger brother who "dabbles" in the market).

You can begin by taking a course (for example, Understanding the Financial Page or Retirement Planning) at an adult education center. Numerous banks, to encourage women investors, offer evening lectures or a series of seminars. These programs are usually free.

You can also find the information you need right on the shelves of your library. Money management (investing, tax planning, home buying) books are in demand as the population tries to figure out how to stretch their dollars.

Getting Professional Advice

There are professionals who earn their money just by advising you on ways to part with yours.

A *CPA* (Certified Public Accountant) can figure out your income tax and prepare the necessary forms, advise on ways to reduce future tax bills, and check your bank statements. He or she can also explain available tax breaks if you are thinking of selling your home or if you own rental property. (If your financial picture is fairly simple, with no drastic changes in income, you can prepare your own taxes with the help of your local IRS [Internal Revenue Service] office. Free assistance is offered in person and over the phone.)

Banking personnel can help you attain financing (if you are buying a residence or returning to school) and advise you on bank products such as certificates of deposit (CDs) and Individual Retirement Accounts (IRAs). There is no charge for these services. There is a charge if you choose to keep your important papers, documents, and valuables in a bank's safe-deposit box. (Yearly rental ranges from ten to fifty dollars depending on the size of the box.)

A *stockbroker* can work out an investment plan whereby you will get the best total return on your money. You can invest in growth stocks, bonds, mutual funds, and tax shelters. How much money are you willing to risk? How much do you need? The more open you are about your financial considerations, the better advice you will receive. A commission will be charged each time the broker buys and/or sells for your account. There are more than 450 brokerage firms with membership in the New York Stock Exchange. Since entrance standards for the exchange are high, be sure the firm you choose is a member.

The *Certified Financial Planner* is there to analyze your complete financial picture and make appropriate recommendations. Satisfied clients cite higher income, lower taxes, and an increase in their assets. (CFPs are a relatively new source for professional advice. As you would with any consultant, do your homework by carefully checking the individual's credentials.)

Obtaining Credit

"I never realized how hard it was to get credit," bemoaned Andrea, sixty-three, "until after my divorce. Nothing was in my name. I was forced to start all over again." To build a credit rating, you should do the following:

☐ Obtain a department store charge card and pay your bills on time.

□ Open a savings and/or checking account.
□ Become acquainted with your bank president or vice-president.

The Equal Credit Opportunity Act prohibits discrimination in granting credit on the basis of sex, age, or marital status.

If you are turned down for credit (denied a loan or not accepted for a charge card), you have the right to know why, as spelled out in the Fair Credit Reporting Act. Do the following:

□ Ask for a written explanation of the denial. The creditor must respond within thirty days.
□ Obtain the name and address of the credit reporting company. You have the right to that information.
□ Check your credit file. Note incomplete or incorrect information. Make corrections. If the credit company disputes your information, you have the opportunity to write your version and have it placed in your file.

Obtaining credit is a privilege. If you get in over your head (you can't repay your debts), get help. "Credit buying," said Dr. Joyce Brothers, "is much like being drunk. The buzz happens immediately, and it gives you a lift . . . the hangover comes the day after."

If *your* hangover persists, contact your creditors. Make a plan for restitution and stick to it. If your financial problems are overwhelming, a consumer credit counseling service can help you with budget planning and money management. The counseling is usually free.

Insurance

What about insurance? Do you really need it? Do you have too much or not enough? Insurance is financial protection against an unexpected event or loss. What you are buying is some degree of security if the unexpected happens—to your health, life, home, personal property, or car. An insurance policy, like any legal contract, is a minefield of terms and clauses. Don't accept your agent's word for what is included and what is not. Read your policy. Have a dictionary by your elbow if necessary. It is important that you understand your coverage.

Do you know the location of your present insurance policies? Have you reviewed these policies within the last year? Has there been a change in your beneficiaries? Do you know the cash, loan, and other conversion values? Do you need to buy more insurance or cash in those policies you have?

The American Council of Life Insurance suggests you make sure your beneficiaries understand your policy or policies. The council also advises you to keep your policies at home and the company name and policy numbers in a safe-deposit box.

The following brief explanations of insurance coverage are only a jumping-off point to your own investigation.

If you are single and have no dependents, you probably don't need *life insurance*. You need to ask yourself who would suffer financially if you died. (For instance, are you contributing to the support of an aged sister?) Perhaps the money you would put into premiums could be invested somewhere else.

"Whole life" insurance (also known as ordinary life and straight life) upon death will pay survivors a benefit and will maintain your dependents' standard of living. If *you* live long enough, it will also pay something to you. You can borrow against the cash value of the policy, but you will be charged interest.

Term insurance is temporary (it may be renewable annually) coverage to a certain age or for a set amount of years. (Numerous policies have a cutoff at sixty-five or seventy years.) There is no cash value built up, and you cannot borrow against the policy. This policy is convertible, meaning you can exchange it for another plan.

Disability insurance coverage is sometimes provided under group life/health insurance. If you are disabled or unable to work because of illness, the insurance benefits will substitute for your income.

Endowment insurance includes both insurance and cash benefits. The focus appears to be more on savings than on protection. The face amount of the policy is paid during your lifetime on a date determined by you (the maturity date). The premiums may run quite high.

Homeowners' insurance is needed to insure your house for at least 80 percent of its replacement cost. The contents (furniture, appliances, etc.) are insured at the same figure. A liability clause will insure you if someone is injured on your premises.

If you rent a house or an apartment, ask your insurance agent about a tenants' policy. This special coverage will insure your personal belongings and also provide liability protection.

"Riders" are provisions added to your original policy (for example, insuring valuables such as a favorite piece of jewelry).

With today's astronomical medical costs, it is essential to cover yourself as thoroughly as possible through *medical insurance*. Learn what is reimbursed to you or your doctor. Are you covered for hospitalization, laboratory tests, office visits, surgical fees, and prescriptions? Be sure you understand your deductibles. (A deductible is a set amount *you* pay before the policy begins to pay you for expenses incurred. A typical plan might pay 80 percent of each loss above a deductible amount, for example, $100.00. Then you pay the other 20 percent.

An *HMO* (Health Maintenance Organization) provides a plan for complete medical care for one fixed annual fee. Drugs may or may not be included. The doctors you choose to see (physicians and specialists) must be members of the HMO. Note whether they participate in Medicare (see page 134).

(If you are between fifty and sixty-five and still working, you might be interested in the health insurance coverage offered by the American Association of Retired Persons. For information, write AARP, 1909 K Street, NW, Washington, DC 20049. If you are over sixty-five, AARP has numerous medical plans to choose from. Details and charges can be obtained from AARP, Group Health Insurance Program, PO Box 13999, Philadelphia, PA 19187.)

There are more than 1,800 insurance companies in the United States. One of them will surely fit your needs. (One might turn down your application while another company will be happy to issue a policy.)

And don't forget to look into the group insurance plans offered by your work place or to ask about coverage from organizations to which you belong.

To check out any company that interests you, consult *Best's Insurance Guide* (published by an insurance rating service), available in most public libraries.

Medicare is a federal program of health insurance for Americans sixty-five years old or older. It is divided into two parts. Part A covers hospital costs for short-term illnesses of up to sixty days in a semiprivate room. (There is a deductible of $400.00.) Part A does not include coverage for items such as doctors' fees, private-duty nursing, or the first three pints of blood.

Part B of Medicare is optional. For a monthly fee of $15.20, you are entitled to see doctors and obtain other medical services as an outpatient. (You pay the first $75.00 in fees.) Medicare then pays 80 percent of the "approved amount" by federal standards for a particular service. Part B does not include routine physical examinations, prescription or nonprescription medications, and dental care, among other services.

To get total value from your Medicare plan, choose your doctors wisely. Ask if they accept Medicare assignments *before* you go for treatment. (This means that your bill will not be more than the amount approved by Medicare.) As you would with other insurance claims, keep accurate records, complete all forms, and hold on to correspondence.

Yes, there are gaps in Medicare insurance. And, yes, you might want to look into other policies. But don't let yourself be scared into buying additional coverage without doing some comparison shopping. (Blue Cross/Blue Shield plans may be a viable standard of measurement.)

Insurance coverage under *Medicaid* is available to those who meet state income requirements. There is no age limit. State benefits may vary, but services such as hospitalization and diagnostic and preventive examinations are included. To apply, contact your local welfare or Social Security office.

Social Security

Ah, Social Security, the big one. To qualify, you must be at least sixty-two years old for early retirement with reduced benefits. If you wait till you are sixty-five, you should file for your benefits approximately three months before you plan to retire. Contact your local Social Security office (listed in the telephone book) to obtain information. No one will call on you. *You* must take the initiative.

The regulations on work and benefit payments is as follows: If you work between ages sixty-two and seventy, there are limits placed on your earnings. If you go over these limits, you will incur a penalty. After age seventy, the sky's the limit on your earning potential— without penalty.

The Social Security Administration says that of the 32.2 million adults receiving benefits, about three out of five are women. And if you study the regulations, you will see how we have been shortchanged, with systematic discrimination. For instance, benefits are based on a traditional earning scale (for every dollar earned by a male, a female earns fifty-nine cents) that is sex-biased. In addition, if you left the labor force to raise a family, there will be gaps in your Social Security record. And if you did work steadily, the likelihood of receiving a private pension on retirement is quite small (80 percent of all retirement-age women have no access to private pensions). If you did not work, you are further penalized if your marriage lasted less than ten years. These are just a few of the inequities that groups like National Organization for Women (NOW), the Older Women's League (OWL), the American Association of Retired Persons (AARP), and the Gray Panthers are working to change.

The first thing to do on retirement is to learn the full extent of your benefits. And then, as Tish Sommers of OWL urges, "Don't agonize. Organize!" If women don't band together to fight for their entitlements, who will?

Planning Retirement

Now is the time to preserve your capital, to review your needs, and to stick to your *budget*. Financial columnist Robert S. Rosefsky advises midlife singles to calculate their specific dollar needs on retirement. With that sum in mind, deduct Social Security payments, pension, and/or annuity income. What's the difference? Can it be made up through savings? Have you figured a cost-of-living increase? Knowing how much you will need should be an impetus to future planning. This is the moment for lots of paper-and-pencil work. List *all* expenses, all income. Do you come out short? What can you cut out? What can you do to get the amounts in sync?

Investments

How about investments as a tool for saving? For those of you who don't want to worry about managing money or about outliving your income, annuities could be a solution. You would pay a lump sum to an insurance company in return for a guaranteed income paid out over time during your life. A deferred annuity is paid out at a date or age in the future.

Other investments to consider include growth stocks, bonds, mutual funds, money market funds, and certificates of deposit.

Joseph L. Oppenheimer, vice-president of Standard & Poor's Corporation, an investment information and advisory service, cautioned, "No single investment is suitable for all people at all times." He suggests that you divide your money and ignore anyone who promises a get-rich-quick scheme. "To be a wise investor," he counseled, "you need to ask questions. Don't be embarrassed. You worked hard for your money. Work just as hard learning how to put it to work."

There has been widespread publicity on the Individual Retirement Account (IRA). For an older working woman, it makes good sense as an investment. You can put up to $2,000 of earned income each year into an IRA without paying taxes on this sum—until you decide to make a withdrawal. Regulations concern age. There is a penalty and income tax due if you withdraw your money before age 59½. But you must withdraw by age 70½. You might want to divide your $2,000 and open a number of accounts.

The Keogh pension plan is primarily for those who are self-employed. It has all the benefits of the IRA, and the dollar amount is up to $30,000 or 25 percent of net earned income, whichever is less. A self-employed person can have both a Keogh and an IRA.

The IRA and Keogh are available at banks, savings

and loans, brokerage firms, and insurance companies. Search for the highest interest rates.

Guidelines for New Widows

"When Dave died," said Sarah, sixty-one, "I was devastated. Money was the last thing on my mind." There's no doubt that widowhood is traumatic. But I urge you to pull yourself together and take the necessary steps to ensure *your* future.

Financial columnist Bonnie Siverd recommends the following guidelines for taking control.

1. Track down your husband's will.
2. Pinpoint your husband's assets.
3. Line up at least twenty copies of the death certificate.
4. Claim any life insurance payments.
5. File for Social Security benefits.
6. Transfer titles of jointly held property.
7. Draw up a financial plan and budget.
8. Revise your will or draw one up if you have none.
9. Protect your credit record.
10. Polish your money skills.

Don't let your personal loss escalate into a financial one!

Wills

Sandy, sixty-four, was afraid to make a will. "It feels so . . . final. If I sign one, I'll die." "But what happens," I asked, "without one?" "Well," she said, making a face, "I guess my things are up for grabs."

First, I've never heard of anyone who signed a will, put down the pen, and keeled over from the act of putting a name to paper.

Second, if there is no will, the state will dispose of your things according to law. This is known as dying intestate. Would you rather have the gold locket you've worn for years be given to your favorite niece or become the property of the state? Laws vary on who gets what and how much, though family members usually become the heirs. (Imagine dying without a will and your beloved house going to a younger brother you haven't spoken to in over a decade?) Your estate includes all your property—furniture, clothing, jewelry, books, and so on. A will will ensure distribution according to *your* wishes.

A will, one of the easiest documents to prepare, should be drawn up by a lawyer. In it, you name an executor (friend, relative, or lawyer) who will be responsible for carrying out your instructions. Your lawyer will keep the original. You take a copy of the will and put it in a secure place (not in a safe-deposit box, since these are sometimes sealed until they can be inventoried by the state). Tell one other person where you have put it. Review your will once a year. Bring any additions or changes to the attention of your lawyer.

Estelle, seventy-four, drew up a "friendship will." Another woman I know calls hers a "sentimental will." Whatever the name, the message and intent is the same, to leave your possessions to friends and relatives who would enjoy them. Do you have a set of dishes you love? a collection of books that have meaning? List those people to whom you would like to leave tangible memories of your existence.

Item	Person It Goes To
collection of detective novels	*Shirley*

In addition, Concern for Dying, an educational council, has prepared a living will (see page 140). "This document enables individuals, while competent, to give their directions for treatment during terminal illness, including the withholding or withdrawal of life-support systems."

The wills cited aim to offer protection before a crisis occurs. They offer a measure of control while you are still in charge of your life.

Power of Attorney

One last financial issue to be aware of is a power of attorney. This is a legal document, drawn up by a lawyer, designating someone to act in your behalf when you may be unable to do so (if you're traveling, disabled, or hospitalized). You may choose to have your representative take responsibility for signing checks, selling real estate, or buying property in your name. This is a considerable power to turn over to someone else, so choose wisely.

Record Keeping

Some words on record keeping: Keep records! Make lists of charge accounts, credit cards, policy numbers, bank accounts, deeds, stock and bond certificates, and so on. Know where you can put your hands on any piece of paper relevant to your financial picture. You can use file folders, large manila envelopes—anything that will keep all your material in some organized fashion.

Credit Cards	Account Number
Visa (Chase Manhattan Bank)	*9999999*

To My Family, My Physician, My Lawyer and All Others Whom It May Concern

Death is as much a reality as birth, growth, maturity and old age—it is the one certainty of life. If the time comes when I can no longer take part in decisions for my own future, let this statement stand as an expression of my wishes and directions, while I am still of sound mind.

If at such a time the situation should arise in which there is no reasonable expectation of my recovery from extreme physical or mental disability, I direct that I be allowed to die and not be kept alive by medications, artificial means or "heroic measures". I do, however, ask that medication be mercifully administered to me to alleviate suffering even though this may shorten my remaining life.

This statement is made after careful consideration and is in accordance with my strong convictions and beliefs. I want the wishes and directions here expressed carried out to the extent permitted by law. Insofar as they are not legally enforceable, I hope that those to whom this Will is addressed will regard themselves as morally bound by these provisions.

(Optional specific provisions to be made in this space)

DURABLE POWER OF ATTORNEY (optional)

I hereby designate _____ to serve as my attorney-in-fact for the purpose of making medical treatment decisions. This power of attorney shall remain effective in the event that I become incompetent or otherwise unable to make such decisions for myself.

Optional Notarization:	Signed_____
"Sworn and subscribed to	Date _____
before me this _____ day	Witness_____
of _____, 19_____."	Witness_____

_____
Notary Public
(seal)

Copies of this request have been given to _____

_____ _____

(Optional)   My Living Will is registered with Concern for Dying (No. _____)

Reprinted with the permission of Concern for Dying, 250 West 57th St., New York, NY 10107.

There are no easy answers to questions regarding money. The best way to handle your financial life is to be aware of all of your options and to obtain professional advice if needed. If you plan for your financial future—if you assure yourself some cushion of comfort—you will be able to enter your later years with expectation rather than with dread.

―――――――――――

Sally Sterman is a sixty-seven-year-old CPA who has her own business, teaches accounting, and runs financial consciousness-raising groups. Tall and blond, she was wearing a soft rose-colored suit with a beige silk blouse when we met.

"I got into accounting really by accident. I'd married rather young and still wanted to finish college. I transferred from day sessions to evening sessions. At that time Hunter College only had a few courses available in my major—which was home economics, believe it or not. So I said, 'What the devil, I'll take accounting courses.' And I did well. I was always the only woman in the class, and I never received too much encouragement from the professors. Fortunately, there was one woman professor who became my mentor, and she urged me to take the CPA curriculum and the CPA exam, which I did.

"Work is an important part of my life. I think it's a part where you can grow and mature at your own pace. I've worked as an employee in several kinds of firms as a woman accountant during the years when it was still very new. I was the recipient of the usual macho discriminatory treatment that's been handed out to so many women. And I felt I was never able to get the recognition that I thought I should have. In one particular job, the very last one I had, I managed a twenty-five-person accounting department. When I asked for the title of controller, I was turned down. I was okay as long as I was an office manager or an accounting manager, but no title and no decent salary. I know that's changed for women today—

maybe not totally to one's satisfaction, but a great deal. So in 1976 I decided I was going to see how I'd do in business for myself. Although there are many women accountants now, they still haven't made that jump or that leap into going out on their own. What's characteristic about the accounting profession is that it's relatively easy to establish one's own practice. There are a lot of men who do it, but unfortunately women still do not.

"How do I get my clients? Well, I join organizations and talk to people. In fact my very first client I picked up in my beauty shop the day I had my cards printed. I decided I'd go to everybody who was in the beauty shop and hand out my cards, and there was an entrepreneur there who had a little boutique, and she said, 'Oh, I need an accountant, and I don't want to use my husband's because I don't want them to know what's happening with my business.' And that started it. I'll go to an ophthalmologist, and I'll tell him about my eye problems and why I have them, because I'm an accountant, and he says, 'Oh, by the way, I need an accountant.' That happens to me a lot. The need is certainly there. I'd say that the whole area of discrimination and the macho stuff that one feels when one's in a corporation working with people, I've almost eliminated. I no longer have to deal with it because the people who come into my office know I'm a woman. They've been referred by someone who's informed them, so it simply doesn't enter into it. Occasionally a female client will get married or take a male partner, and I'll be replaced. It's okay. I can live with it.

"My fun is really my work. I think accounting is really a helping, a servicing, profession, and people who need financial help or who need help in getting their finances in order respond very readily to my own personal characteristics, many of which stem from being a woman with a lifetime of raising a family and doing all the things that so many women have done. I think I bring a little more patience. I think my communication is a little bit better. And I do—especially for new business owners—a little bit more hand holding than other accountants do or think about or know about or want to do.

"I think the best way to choose an accountant is through a referral. It's a good idea to get at least three or four names. Then I'd interview each of them. I think the choice should be made on the ability of the accountant to communicate because, really, the practice of accounting is the communication of financial information. Accountants have the reputation of being uptight and tight-lipped. It means they don't talk. They tend to be very rigid. They get caught up with being 'very professional.' They emulate to some degree the kind of behavior that many doctors are accused of. They don't really tell a patient what's happening and why. And that's detrimental to the patient—and to the accountant's client.

"I think women have got to give up thinking that someone else can or should help them. Translation means you've got to accept responsibility for your own finances, and that really is a monumental step. It's not something you grow into; you have to switch gears and say, 'I'm going to be responsible for my own financial well-being.' And from that thought you'll arrive at the ways to do it.

"I've done a series of financial consciousness-raising groups, mostly for women because women really feel comfortable with a financial advisor. One of the first things I say to them is, 'Never ask me a dumb question, because if you ask a dumb question, then I'm a dummy, and I'm not a dummy.' But there's no such thing as a naive question, and I think to men there is. They say, 'Dear, dear,' or 'Don't worry about it,' or 'This is too complicated.' I never assume that. And it works because women do want to know. They do want to understand, but if they keep running into these patronizing attitudes, it may take them longer to get with it. I generally find the level of financial awareness in women rising, and that's gratifying.

"My daughter is forty, and my son is thirty-seven. They're both married. My daughter works with me.

I'm training her. She's very interested in the firm. My son is involved in setting up his own restaurant, and he's relying on me for guidance and financial advice. It makes me very happy to be able to give them the best of what I've accumulated during the past twenty years.

"There's a satisfaction that's come to me because of what I've done that I call power. I'm not referring to it as power over other people but a power over your own life. I recommend it.

"The best thing about being single is growing up and standing on my own two feet. I've been divorced twice. There just aren't enough men in my age group who can deal with a woman on an equal level. In my particular case it's because I'm in a profession, and men in my generation, well, it scares the hell out of them. It scared the hell out of my last husband. They can't deal with it. I find younger men are much better in that regard.

"I just lost thirty pounds. I went on a protein diet under the direction of a doctor. It's done wonders for me. And maybe one of these days I'll go in for plastic surgery and see if I can't drop off another five years from my appearance. I think it's in our own best interests to look as good as we possibly can. And when you look in a mirror and you look good, it feels good. It's great.

"In regard to my future, I'm expanding. I'm going to get my credentials for Certified Financial Planner. I start taking courses in September. And that should keep me occupied well into my ninth decade!"

For More Information

Organizations

National Consumer Insurance Organization
344 Commerce Street
Alexandria, VA 22314

International Association for Financial Planning (IAFP)
5775 Peachtree Dunwoody Road, NE, Suite 120C
Atlanta, GA 30342
(for lists of financial planners in your area)

Institute of Certified Financial Planners
3443 South Galena, Suite 190
Denver, CO 80231
(for information and referrals)

CO$T (Committee of Single Taxpayers)
1628 21st Street, NW
Washington, DC 20009
(nonprofit, nonpartisan organization to rectify inequities in
tax structure that discriminate against singles)

The Pension Rights Center
932 Dupont Circle Building
Washington, DC 20036

National Foundation for Consumer Credit
8701 Georgia Avenue, Suite 601
Silver Springs, MD 20910

Women's Credit & Finance Project
PO Box 10789
Marina del Rey, CA 90295

Zonta International
35 E. Wacker Drive
Chicago, IL 60601
(for information on investment counseling)

National Women's Political Caucus
1411 K Street, NW
Washington, DC 20005
(Older Women's Division offers information and workshops
on financial matters.)

Publications

Estimating Your Social Security Retirement Check; Thinking About Retiring; SSI for Aged, Disabled, and Blind People; A Woman's Guide to Social Security; and *Guide to Health Insurance for People with Medicare.* Available from your local Social Security office. No charge.

Consumer Handbook to Credit Protection Laws. Send to Board of Governors of the Federal Reserve System, Washington, DC 20551.

Your Vital Papers Logbook. May be ordered for a fee from AARP, 1909 K Street, NW, Washington, DC 20049.

Your Pension Rights at Divorce. Send $2.00 and a self-addressed business envelope to The Pension Rights Center, 932 Dupont Circle Building, Washington, DC 20036.

Books

Brien, Mimi. *Moneywise.* New York: Bantam Books, 1982.

Chasen, Nancy H. *Policy Wise.* Washington, DC: AARP; Glenview, Ill.: Scott, Foresman & Co., 1983. (An AARP Book)

Miller, Theodore J., ed. *Making Your Money Grow.* New York: Dell Publishing Co., 1981.

Porter, Sylvia. *Sylvia Porter's New Money Book for the 80's.* New York: Avon Books, 1980.

Simon, Dyanne Asimow. *The Barter Book.* New York: E. P. Dutton, 1979.

Siverd, Bonnie. *Count Your Change: A Woman's Guide to Sudden Financial Change.* New York: Arbor House Publishing, 1983.

9

Your Working Self

In order that people may be happy in their work, these three things are needed: They must be fit for it; They must not do too much of it; And they must have a sense of success in it.

—John Ruskin

Gerontologist Dr. Alex Comfort has said regarding retirement, "Two weeks is about the ideal length of time to retire." If you agree, begin to formulate your plans *before* you leave your present position. If you want to stay in your field, examine the opportunities for part-time or consulting work. Make the contacts and lay the groundwork while you still have a base of power and responsibility.

"The last six months on my job I must have given my business card to over a hundred people," said Miranda, sixty-three, who took early retirement. "I pushed myself to be out there, to make myself known to anyone who might want my advice in the future." Miranda, a former book publicist, now has in addition to her authors, accounts that include a charity organization, a chamber music group, and a chain of small boutiques. "Being on my own made me branch out, to look for and make my opportunities."

Preretirement Planning

If you have some idea of what you want to be doing in the future, something different from your present job, start your preparation *now*. See if your dreams can be turned into reality. By trying them out while you still have a safety net, you'll be able to make an informed decision on retirement. So, take courses, talk to people, and read.

Consider your reasons for working.

I *want* to work because _____

_____

_____

_____

_____

I *need* to work because _____

_____

_____

_____

_____

Career Counseling

If you have no plans, if you are tired of volunteer jobs, if you have to get a job because of financial need, or if you've had no past work history, you might want to consult a career counselor. Be clear on one fact: A career counselor will not and should not guarantee you a job. She or he can, with your input (through written and verbal exercises), help you define your goals and use your history and your present needs to narrow the search. In later counseling sessions you can learn how to prepare a resume and cover letter, develop job-hunting strategies and marketing techniques, and role-play that all-important job interview.

Ruth Shapiro, of Ruth Shapiro Associates in New York, is a career counselor with ten years of experience. Having worked with hundreds of women, she sees the counseling role as a collaboration. In choosing someone to work with, Ms. Shapiro stressed that aside from credentials such as a master's degree in vocational guidance and counseling and references, there should be a sense of rapport. "Do you trust this person?" asked Ms. Shapiro.

To find a career counselor, you can look in the Yellow Pages; contact your local Y, community center, university, or community college; or write to Catalyst (see page 159) for their nationwide list of professionals.

Older Workers and Jobs

Did you know that numerous modeling agencies are beginning to open divisions that feature older models (gray hair is in!)? And some employment agencies have been following suit (for example, Mature Temps, a division of Temps America).

You may or may not find such a specialized agency. If you don't, try to find one that targets your job interest. There are agencies that specialize in financial positions, some for ex-teachers, and some just for temporary work (a day or week at a time). See if you can work with one particular person rather than report to several. And give this person feedback. Was the job appropriate for your level of skill? Was the interviewer pleasant? Was there any age-bias? Don't sign any contract regarding fees until you have read it carefully and understand the provisions. If you feel that a particular person is not doing his or her job in helping to find one of your own, speak to the manager or supervisor of the agency. You will, of course, be on time for all your appointments.

If you can do the job, why should your age be a factor? It shouldn't, of course, but out there in the real world some people equate numbers, over half a hundred, with inability, incompetence, or worse.

Flash! Numerous studies have come out *in favor* of the older worker for these reasons.

- ☐ Absenteeism is lower than that of younger workers.
- ☐ Productivity is the same or higher.
- ☐ Workers are more attentive to job performance.
- ☐ Greater stability exists with turnover more than 60 percent or less than for younger employees.
- ☐ Adjectives to describe the older worker included *dependable, adaptable, seasoned, mature, loyal, responsible,* and *confident.*

Discrimination based on age is ageism. Job/career specialist Shirley Sloan Fader urged readers of *Working Woman* magazine to "avoid telling your age. Just write 'over 40' in the age space on your application. And give the same response, if asked your age, during the interview."

Ms. Shapiro voiced objection to the issue of age. "Age or personal information does not belong on a resume. It only feeds into possible prejudice." (This includes no dates of college graduation and no ages of children.) She suggests that an applicant reply to the question of age with the question, How does this relate to the specific responsibilities of the job?

It seems ironic—doesn't it?—that the very years that make you qualified for a position work against you in obtaining it.

Merrell Clark, president of Elderworks, sees a positive trend for people in the second half of life who want to remain in or enter the job force. Elderworks is involved with the community groups and educational institutions to promote career opportunities for older people. "The ideal," said Mr. Clark, "would be that every corporation would have in mind a percentage of older people to hire, a recruitment service to match these job specifications, and demand that would lead supply." Obviously something to work for!

The Executive Volunteer Corps of New York City offers free expert business and financial advice to anyone who walks in the door. All the counselors are retired volunteers with years of diverse business experience. Marty Schwartz, the counselor I talked with, is sixty-two. "We might have someone come in who has recently started a business and is having trouble. Could be a cash flow problem, some difficulty with the landlord or with a partner, or perhaps a need for advertising. Some people come in for us to go over their books, to see if the accounts are being kept correctly."

When asked about the opportunities for a woman in her own business, Mr. Schwartz replied that they were out there but that you had to know what you were doing. "Despite all the other variables," he cautioned, "if you don't have the money and experience, it won't be a go. It's not enough to like dresses if you're thinking of opening a dress shop."

Your city may have its own Executive Volunteer Corps. The Small Business Administration (SBA) oversees two such similar organizations: SCORE (Senior Corps of Retired Executives) and ACE (Active Corps of Executives). You can find their phone numbers in your telephone book.

The Senior Community Service Employment Program (SCSEP) has offices in thirty-five states. Sponsored by the American Association of Retired Persons, the program is designed to (1) re-skill disadvantaged older persons for entry into the nation's labor force, (2) demonstrate that older persons who may have been considered unemployable have much to offer employers in the public and private sectors, and (3) train older persons in job search techniques.

To qualify for a work experience (temporary job-training position), you must be fifty-five years of age or older and have an income no higher than the Department of Labor standard for economically disadvantaged persons.

The program's long-range goal is to help older people find permanent or part-time positions such as hospital aides, drivers, receptionists, typists, telephone operators, and day-care workers.

Displaced Homemaker

Either you have lived it or you know someone who has. Woman A married at nineteen, raised three children, cooked, cleaned, was the perfect hostess for a young lawyer on the rise. Thirty-five years later. The lawyer is a partner in his law firm and lives with a woman twenty years his junior who is pregnant. Woman A is now fifty-four and unemployed with no prospects and can look ahead to, say, some twenty-five more years of productive life. She is divorced with a drastic cut in income, has no viable skills, and is effectively displaced. Where can she turn for help?

One option might be the Displaced Homemaker Program, sponsored by the Department of Labor. This is specifically for women who have lost their in-home employment as mothers and household managers because of divorce, death, or desertion of a spouse. The program's aim is to help women achieve economic independence by providing individual and group counseling (assessment of needs and skills), health education, job training (office skills, resume writing, and so on), financial and legal information (insurance, taxes, estate and probate problems), and placement services.

Mavis Sutton, director of the New York City Re-entry Employment program (formerly called the Displaced Homemaker Program), noted that women who completed the program gained in self-awareness and esteem. The New York course, as a model, offers an eight-week training program that includes three days of workshops and two days of doing volunteer work to gain job experience and a reference for a future paid position. Information is conveyed to past, present, and future members of the program through the newsletter, *Late Bloomer*. Services are provided free of charge.

Evaluating Your Skills

Evaluate yourself. Did you finish high school? college? graduate school? Where did your education stop? (Note that formal learning isn't everything. Life experience, volunteer activities, special talents and skills—all complete the picture.) List everything you have done and can do. Ask yourself how much you have learned, in or out of a classroom, that you can use in applying for a job. Have you traveled? Are you athletic? Do you play a musical instrument? Do you speak a foreign language? Can you arrange flowers? Do you know calligraphy? Can you operate a computer? Do you have an eye for color and detail? Are children drawn to you?

There may be opportunities where your skill is used indirectly. Lois, fifty-seven, prides herself on her gourmet cooking. No, she didn't open a restaurant. "Too much work. I wanted to enjoy myself, not kill myself earning money." Her solution? She found a part-time job demonstrating cooking appliances at her local department store. She gets a chance to cook, to use the latest equipment, to give a "performance," and to meet people. Yes, she's earning money.

Do you cook well enough to cater? dance well enough to teach? Do you write rhymes that can be used for greeting cards? Use your skills and talents to create a job that's uniquely tailored to your interests and personality.

If you are a compulsive organizer and your house and life are in order, go into your community and do it for someone else for an hourly fee. You can put papers in order, organize kitchen and bedroom closets, clean out drawers, and sort books and records.

Are you a fast, accurate typist? Can you work for long hours without back and shoulder problems? You can set up a typing service right in your home and type people's manuscripts, letters, dissertations, resumes, and bills.

Are you assertive? aggressive? able to stand up to salesmen? Some of us are, and some of us would rather just forget the whole thing. You can help those in the latter group by complaining on *their* behalf. You can return merchandise, obtain refunds, and have bills corrected.

And if you like to shop, there's a way to do it without spending any of *your* money. Do it for someone else. You can shop for clothes, groceries, household items, appliances, and presents.

And what about renting your services as a care-taker? Take charge for those people who go on vacation. You can house-sit, water plants, collect the mail, and feed the pets.

The *New York Times* recently reported on a service for people who hate to wait in lines. They have people who do it for you! If you don't mind standing around and enjoy the opportunity to be surrounded by others, this could be a job for you. You can stand in line to obtain someone's passport, renew a driver's license, pay a traffic ticket, and order theater tickets.

What are your strengths? How can you take those strengths and spin them off into a business?

What I Do Well	How I Can Use It
embroidery	*samplers*
	tablecloths
	handkerchiefs

What I Do Well (continued)	**How I Can Use It**
_____	_____
	_____
	_____
_____	_____
	_____
	_____
_____	_____
	_____
	_____
_____	_____
	_____
	_____
_____	_____
	_____
	_____
_____	_____
	_____
	_____

Networking

Barbara calls Sue for the name of her eye doctor. Sue says he's on vacation, but *her* friend Ruta has one she swears is terrific. Sue gives Barbara Ruta's phone number.

Gloria meets Nell, the wife of a business associate, in the supermarket and asks about her volunteer job. Nell is so enthusiastic that Gloria becomes interested. Nell promises to call her later in the day to give her the name and telephone number of the director of the organization and to personally put in a word on her behalf.

Joan talks to Ruth at a party. They discover they are both former teachers. They exchange phone numbers. Months later Joan gets a call from Ruth, who has set up a tutoring center and needs additional staff. Joan is surprised and delighted to be remembered.

All three situations involve networking, a relatively new concept for women. Men have been networking for years. They have a drink. They talk about deals. They play cards and exchange gossip and career news. They golf and discuss investments. By exchanging information, they help one another move up or along the ladder. Women have just started to network for information, support, and advice and to increase their opportunities for business ventures.

When you network, you enlarge your field of contacts. The more people you meet, the more possibilities for action. You don't have to love or become best friends with the women and men in your network. You do have to keep open the lines of communication. At times you'll be the giver; at other moments you'll be the one who gets back. You can have a social network, a health network, and one for your career, and they can all be interwoven. Networking is a mutual investment plan.

If you are considering a job move (paid or volunteer), think of five people you can call for information and leads. List this network below and refer to it when you have made up your mind.

Name	Phone Number

Starting Your Own Business

Starting your own business can be costly but exciting and possibly lucrative. It involves many variables. To cut down on the risks, do the following:

1. Make sure you are going to like what you have chosen to do.
2. Be prepared for long days and nights (and weekends) of work.
3. Learn about finances or find someone you can trust for this responsibility.
4. Research the competition. If there are three day-care centers in town, how will yours be different?
5. Estimate the amount of money you will need to get your business off the ground. What are the costs of rent, equipment, furnishings, utilities, stationery, and salaries?
6. Calculate how much money you will need for a good trial run (let's say six months).
7. Explore all avenues for financial aid. Can you get a bank loan and/or would you qualify for one from the Women's Business Enterprise program at the SBA?
8. Consult a lawyer or accountant for advice.
9. Don't open the doors until everything—absolutely everything—has been checked and rechecked.
10. Keep a financial record of every single transaction.
11. Try to enjoy yourself in the process.

My first career was teaching children in elementary school. Thirteen years ago I became a free-lance writer. It seemed a glamorous occupation, and I'd be able to leave a little bit of me behind. Getting started wasn't easy. First, there's nothing glamorous about sitting alone in an empty room talking to a blank piece of paper. Although I wished for a good-typing fairy who'd make the right words magically appear, it didn't happen. Biting the bullet, I gave myself a year to "make it." I subscribed to professional magazines (*The Writer, Writer's Digest*), diligently studied *Writer's Market* (the bible of where to sell what), attended two writers' conferences, and wrote every single day. The first article I sold went to an educational magazine. The subject was How to Use Macaroni in Your Classroom. (Write about what you know.) I was paid five dollars and was overjoyed.

Over the years and many, many words later, I realize that one reason I persisted was that no one told me I couldn't. I had a dream, prepared myself as best I could, and plunged ahead. I truly believe that if you want something badly enough, you'll find a way to get it. It may mean going back to school, becoming partners with someone else, and/or giving up other things, but if the desire is strong enough, you'll find a way.

List three "dream jobs."

1. _____
2. _____
3. _____

Choose one. List the steps you'd have to take to get there.

_____
_____
_____
_____
_____
_____
_____
_____

So maybe you won't be a Broadway actress. What about starring in a local theater production? And perhaps 1988 won't be your turn for vice-president. But how about councilwoman or a member of the school board? If your dream is just a hand stretch away, take a deep breath and reach for it! If the distance is longer, hang in for the duration. You can do it!

For More Information

Organizations

Executive Volunteer Corps
41 East 42nd Street
New York, NY 10017

Catalyst
14 East 60th Street
New York, NY 10021

Displaced Homemakers
    Network, National
    Headquarters
1010 Vermont Avenue, NW
Suite 817
Washington, DC 20005
(Enclose a self-addressed, stamped envelope with your request for a referral to a program in your area.)

Elderworks
420 Lexington Avenue,
Room 2605
New York, NY 10170

National Council of Women
    of the U.S.A.
777 United Nations Plaza
New York, NY 10024

National Federation of Business and Professional Women's
    Clubs
2012 Massachusetts Avenue, NW
Washington, DC 20036
(for information on small business projects)

Numerous state and community colleges and universities now have a women's center or a career counseling department. You can contact them for additional job information.

Publications

Women's Handbook and *Checklist for Going into Business* (MA 2.016) from the U.S. Small Business Administration, PO Box 15434, Fort Worth, TX 76119. (A nationwide, toll-free service, the Answer Desk, will answer questions and make appropriate referrals for guidance. Dial 800-368-5855. In Washington, DC, only, call 653-7561.)

Publications (continued)

Federal Information Centers (list of toll-free numbers that will answer your question, supply information, or make referrals). Send for free booklet to General Services Administration, Washington, DC 20405.

Books

Bolles, Richard. *What Color Is Your Parachute?* Berkeley, CA: Ten Speed Press, 1982.

Fader, Shirley Sloan. *From Kitchen to Career.* New York: Stein & Day, 1978.

Foxworth, Jo. *Boss Lady.* New York: Warner Books, 1979.

Lembeck, Ruth. *1,001 Job Ideas for Today's Woman.* New York: Doubleday & Co., 1975.

McCaslin, Barbara S., and Patricia McNamara. *Be Your Own Boss: A Woman's Guide to Planning & Running Her Business.* Englewood Cliffs, N.J.: Prentice-Hall, 1980.

Welch, Mary-Scott. *Networking.* New York: Warner Books, 1981.

10

Continuing Education

The rung of a ladder was never meant to rest upon, but only to hold a man's foot long enough to enable him to put the other somewhat higher.

—Thomas Henry Huxley

A number of years ago I heard a story that I continue to cherish. A fifty-three-year-old woman decided to enter medical school. It was a decision she had put off for many years. A friend who was thinking of her own retirement tried to dissuade her. "It's four years of school, then an internship, perhaps a residency. You won't even begin to practice until you're sixty." And the soon-to-be medical student replied, "I'm going to be sixty anyway. So why shouldn't I be sixty and a doctor?" Why not indeed?

Courses for Credits

Dianne, sixty-three, was one of nine children. She left school for work in order to contribute financially to her family. Now an accomplished artist, she still felt inadequate because she never graduated from high school: "Nobody knew but me, but that was enough. I realized that getting a diploma wouldn't do a thing for me at this stage in my life. It just became a matter of personal pride. So, without telling anyone, I took the GED and passed!" The GED is the General Educational Development examination, which tests your knowledge and skills in five areas: Writing Skills, Social Studies, Science, Reading Skills, and Mathematics. A passing score will reward you with a high-school equivalency certificate. To brush up on these subjects, you can take adult courses at your local high school or study at home with one of the commercially prepared review books (Scott, Foresman; Arco; Barron's—to name a few). For information on testing centers and costs, contact your neighborhood high school or local board of education.

If you want to attend college now (perhaps you started once upon a time and dropped out), you may be eligible to enter and move through at a faster pace if you take the *College Level Examination Program* (CLEP) tests. Here's a chance to put all the knowledge you have learned outside the classroom to getting into one. A passing score results in college credit toward your undergraduate degree. (Make sure the college program that interests you accepts CLEP credit.) There are more than nine hundred CLEP centers in the country, and examinations are given on a frequent basis. There is a charge for each exam you take.

There are over a thousand *community,* or *junior, colleges* in the United States. These offer two-year programs that may either correspond to the first two years of a four-year college or emphasize technical and vocational training. The tuition is usually low. Graduates of the program receive an associate of arts degree. With this in hand, you can then transfer into the third year at a four-year college if you decide to go on.

The *Union of Experimental Colleges* offers innovative programs of interest to older women. You may be able to attend classes at night, to get credit for life experience, and to study in your hometown and attend classes on campus for a short block of time during the year. (Consult the catalogs for Antioch and Goddard, two well-recognized private colleges that offer unusual learning opportunities.)

Numerous colleges are experimenting with *weekend programs*. You attend a certain number of weekends per year, stay in on-campus housing, and attend classes.

The *University Without Walls* offers a personal approach to learning without ever stepping foot on any campus. A learning contract is drawn up and signed by the student, who agrees to complete certain assignments and readings and to accomplish specific goals during a specified period of time. This is discussed and planned with the help of a faculty advisor. Fieldwork may be included in the contract to allow the student to obtain practical experience in the student's area of interest. (One such participating institution is Empire State College, part of the State University of New York.) Your state department of education can refer you to a school involved in this system of learning.

Correspondence courses are offered by more than seventy colleges and universities. You usually have about a year to complete each course, mailing in each lesson in the series on completion. An instructor returns the work with comments and corrections. Correspondence courses allow you to study anywhere you are at any time. You can study for personal enrichment or for credit. (The National University Continuing Education Association publishes the *Independent Study Catalog,* which features a complete list of courses, descriptions, and participating schools. For information and charges, write to NUCEA Book Order Department 4201, Peterson's Guides, PO Box 2123, Princeton, NJ 08540. Ask for Book 1801. Courses that are more technical or vocational in nature may be taken through the National Home Study Council. You can order their free *Directory of Accredited Home Study Schools* from NHSC, 1601 18th Street, NW, Washington, DC 20009.)

Noncredit Courses

If you don't want or need the educational credit, consider auditing classes that interest you. This is a chance to sit in and learn without the pressure of assignments, exams, or grades. You attend when you wish. To audit a class, you usually need to receive permission from the instructor. You can discover which courses are open from the college director of admissions.

Ten years old and thriving, the Elderhostel program provides unpressured learning on college campuses throughout the United States and in Canada, Mexico, Bermuda, Israel, India, Australia, and Europe. Housing is in dormitories; meals are taken in school cafeterias. Most programs begin Sunday evening and end Saturday morning. There are no exams, grades, or homework. The only requirement is one of age. You must be at least sixty years old to attend, or you may go as the "companion" of someone who is at least sixty. Here's a sampling of courses from the Fall '84 catalog: Folk Art of the Southwest and Mexico, given at Cochise Community College in Arizona; Music of Broadway: Yesterday and Today, given at Caldwell College in New Jersey; Survival Skills for the '80's, held at Green Mountain College in Vermont; and Introduction to Computers, at Elon College in North Carolina. There's much, much more to reinforce the program's belief that "retirement does not have to mean withdrawal, that one's later years are an opportunity to enjoy new experiences." See for yourself. Obtain information and a fee schedule from Elderhostel, 100 Boylston Street, Boston, MA 02116.

Costs of Classes

More than twenty-five states have legislation requiring reduced college tuition for older people or, in some cases, a complete waiver. Age eligibility varies from fifty-five to sixty-two. Obtain information directly from your local college or university. Note that there is often a "space available" regulation. This means that the class will first be open to students paying full tuition. If there is room left for additional students, then it's your turn.

For information on scholarships and loans, contact the financial aid office of the school that interests you. Explore the opportunities sponsored by women's groups. Enlist the support of your local librarian. She or he can ease your search for funds by directing you to the right source books. There's money for education and retraining out there; all you have to do is look.

Benefits of Learning

If you are asking yourself why you should go back to school, consider the benefits. Learning can pay off in knowledge, a new career or interest, job advancement, additional friends, and even fun! Don't be the victim of your own age-bias. You're not *too old* to learn both from books and from the other students. In fact, you yourself could be an important source of instruction. How nice if you can share your life experience with others! Intergenerational learning is an exchange. Think about adding your input.

Gloria, fifty-three, just completed her first year as a full-time social work graduate student. A well-paid, highly thought of executive secretary, she made the switch in career plans after many years of thought and, in a sense, practical experience.

"I've done volunteer work all my life. My father died when I was twelve. I took care of two younger sisters, one of whom died of cerebral palsy. For a number of summers I was a counselor at a camp for disabled children.

"I've always been very organized—started as one of those kids who always kept her toys in a large toy chest, books lined up on the shelves, the whole bit. Being a secretary after high school seemed perfect for my personality. I learned to be a good administrator, to delegate responsibility, to be a jump ahead of my bosses. Meanwhile I was going to college at night. It was slow going. I still lived at home. I finally got my degree. It took more than six years. I remember that I enjoyed studying and only wished I had more time to socialize with the other students.

"Over the years, I've been a volunteer at my local hospital, been a Big Sister to two teenage girls, volunteered my Saturdays at a group home for foster children, and started a group for the foster parents.

"Don't get me wrong. I liked being a secretary, but over the years it seemed as if I looked forward to my volunteer jobs more than to the work I was being paid for.

"One day I said to myself, Am I going to be doing this for the rest of my life? I could do it blindfolded. I was competent, efficient, but I felt I was dying inside. All of a sudden I didn't like being so organized, so great at pushing papers. Being with kids, their parents—that was life, changing and unpredictable. And I could see I was making a difference.

"I talked it out with my therapist, who was very supportive. And then my mother died. I never believed she was satisfied with her life, and I guess I didn't want to die knowing I could have done something else with mine but didn't take the chance.

"What's it like? The worst thing is I've had no leisure time. The laundry sits in piles as does the dust. Weekends I'm in the library; nights I'm studying and writing papers. It's incredible how I got back in so fast. The instructors have all been fair. I find I write very slowly, so I've had to ask for extensions on some of my papers—that perfectionist streak coming out again! And my money situation isn't great. None is coming in; everything is going out.

"On the plus side, I thought my age would be more of an issue than it's been. But there are a number of older students in my class, and that's probably now true in other graduate schools throughout the country. Of course, social work may be different than, say, getting an MBA. Social work is a helping profession, so there's a different feel about the people. I see business students as being more competitive, uptight, rigid. I'm probably wrong and shouldn't generalize. Anyway, I've made two good friends, both younger—one married, one single. They have become very important because they are living through all the feelings I'm experiencing—the anxiety, the doubts, the anger, and the emotional churning up of all our own issues, which become triggered through working this first practice year with clients. It's been vital for me to be able to share with them.

"I'm in a study group with three other students. We take turns Xeroxing all the articles we have to read and have strategy sessions at exam time. The last day of classes we all went to the bookstore and bought school T-shirts.

"I'm taking a course in summer school to lighten my course load for next year. That seemed like a sensible idea.

"My biggest complaint is being tired all the time. But I don't think that's related to my age as much as it's involved with the *amount* of work I have.

"Now all those years of organization and of typing reports are paying off. And I take classroom notes in shorthand.

"My social life has gone down the drain. I'm no longer available for lunch. And on weekends I can barely get my chores done before I'm back to studying or longing to be under the covers.

"I keep telling myself the worst is over. I've made the first year. I've gotten through. I know what to expect. The training I'm getting will allow me to work with children, to use myself in the best way possible. I want that paper, those letters after my name. And in another year I'll have it!

"I see the first half of my life as preparation—of growing up and feeling sure enough to take this risk and make a change. And, you know, however difficult this year has been, it's been worth it."

For More Information

Organizations

Council for the Advancement of Experiential Learning
American City Building
Columbia, MD 21044

Adult Education Association of the U.S.A.
810 18th Street, NW
Washington, DC 20036

Publications

Bulletin of Information for Candidates, CLEP, PO Box 592, Princeton, NJ 08540.

Learning Opportunities for Older Persons, Institute of Lifetime Learning, AARP, 1909 K Street, NW, Washington, DC 20049.

Books

Cross, Wilbur, and Carol Florio. *You Are Never Too Old to Learn.* New York: McGraw-Hill Book Co., 1978.

Gross, Ronald. *The Lifelong Learner.* New York: Simon & Schuster, 1977.

11

Housing

Home ought to be our clearinghouse, the place from which we go forth lessoned and disciplined, and ready for life.

—Kathleen Norris

If you are newly single, *stay put*, for at least six months. When you are the one who is left through death or divorce, there is the urge to run away, to start fresh, to put the past behind you. Don't! ("I just wanted to move in the middle of the night—to steal away from the townspeople who were showering me with pity. He was having an affair with his secretary, and it seems I was the last to know. Thank goodness my daughter convinced me to stay," said Allison, sixty-five.)

If you don't deal with the past, the good parts as well as the bad ones, you'll wear the emotional fallout as a second skin. Don't let the memories force you out (until *you* decide to move). Accept the emotions rather than hide from them. (Glenda, seventy, said, "When Harry died, I wanted to walk out the door and never return. Every time I passed the living room, I saw him in his favorite chair. The house *was* Harry— the bookcases he stained, the window shade he never got to fix. He seemed to be in every room. At first the memories were almost too painful to bear. Our neighborhood, where we lived for twenty-five years, came to my rescue. I later wondered how I ever even considered moving. I needed the house and the people who were part of my past to help me evaluate the future.")

Solo Options

If you *do* decide to move, what are your housing options?

Home ownership. This can be viewed as a financial investment (with tax breaks for mortgage interest costs). It is an advantage for those who enjoy gardening and making home improvements. It provides a sense of roots in the community, a feeling of permanence. It generally means ample space for overnight visits from children and grandchildren. You may feel that being a homeowner gives you an increase in status.

Rental apartment. When you rent, someone else will take care of the taxes, maintenance, and repairs. You are responsible for rent and monthly utilities.

Condominium (condo). The apartment complex is owned by the condominium owners' association, of which you, as the owner of your apartment, are a member. You pay taxes on your unit. Maintenance and security of the common area are taken care of, and you are charged for these services.

Cooperative (co-op). You buy shares (determined by the size and location of your apartment) in the corporation that owns your building. (You do not own your unit, as in a condo.) The corporation is responsible for taxes. There is a board of directors that sometimes sets policy for the building, for example, limits to structural design.

Retirement community. This usually has sports facilities and an ongoing program of social activities.

People are generally of retirement age. Some communities have restrictions regarding children.

Retirement home or hotel. Leave the cooking and cleaning to the staff. Some facilities have medical care available on a twenty-four-hour basis. Aside from those that offer rentals, there are residences that require you to turn over all your assets in exchange for care for the rest of your life. (Investigate this last option carefully.)

Motor home. This is an option for those still on the move. Most consist of a compact living room, dining room, sleeping area, shower compartment, and bathroom. You can settle down for periods of time in trailer parks across the country.

Mobile home. Not all mobile homes are on the highway. Many are permanently situated in special parks where you rent the parking lot. There are usually recreational areas available. A mobile home can be an economical, low-maintenance housing option.

Geographical Areas to Consider

The lures of warm climate, good economic value, and healthy living are drawing many singles to the Sunbelt—the states bordered on the west by California and on the east by North Carolina.

The authors of *Planning Your Retirement Housing* surveyed over a thousand retirees and found the "most expensive metropolitan area for retirement living to be Boston, followed closely by New York City, Seattle, Washington, D.C., San Francisco, and Buffalo." The best bet for your retirement dollars, the least costly metropolitan area, is Atlanta, Georgia.

Decision to Move

Should you move? This is a big step, so very carefully think through the decision.

To Move (For)

1. Neighborhood changing.
_____
_____
_____
_____
_____
_____

Or Not to Move (Against)

1. Will miss children/a two-hour plane ride away.
_____
_____
_____
_____
_____

Before you move, obtain all the information you can find on your new community. Call the Chamber of Commerce, speak to real estate agents, and read the local newspapers. Cover these points.

☐ climate
☐ cost of living
☐ medical care
☐ transportation
☐ recreational facilities
☐ cultural events
☐ shopping
☐ religious institutions
☐ singles population
☐ job opportunities
   (part-time, free-lance)
☐ crime rate/safety aspects

Try to spend some time in your new community before you move. Native Floridians call the people who come to their state during the winter months snowbirds. Lucy, sixty-two, was one from Minneapolis. "I spent four months a year in Miami for three years before I made it my home. I rented an apartment and had plenty of time to look around, to make friends, to see where I'd be most comfortable. I wound up buying a condo a mile from where I was renting."

Options with Someone

If you want to stay in the house or apartment that suddenly is too large and too costly for a single, perhaps the answer is a roommate. If this seems a viable solution, be clear on your motives. Do you crave companionship, or are you just in need of an additional source of rent? Know what you want and expect from a roommate. State your intentions. To find a roommate, you can place an ad or spread the word to friends, relatives, and local community agencies, for example, the neighborhood senior citizens center.

If you don't want to share your apartment or house space with someone on a daily basis but need or want additional income, B and B (Bed and Breakfast) programs may be an answer. (Check into current zoning ordinances in your area; you might need to work to bring about some changes in the regulations.) Farla Zammit, president of the referral service, New Yorkers at Home, estimates two hundred such organizations across the country. As president, Ms. Zammit inspects every home and/or apartment to see the facilities. (Do you have a twin bed? Is it queen-sized? Does the room have a view? Are you near transportation? What about cultural or recreational resources?) She also tries to get a sense of each person as a potential host. (Do you like people? Are you willing to share some of your knowledge about your city with an out-of-towner?) As a host, you may have visitors for two days, no one for a week, and then someone in for a month. You provide the room, linens, and a continental breakfast. Your fee is from twenty-five dollars to fifty dollars a night, depending on the size and location of your apartment. For the guest it's an alternative to hotel living. For you it's a way to earn money and meet a wide variety of people. Guests are asked for references.

Alternative Living for the Aging (ALA) is a non-profit organization whose goal is "to provide shared housing opportunities for older people as an alternative to living alone or living in an institution." Co-op House I, a two-story house in Los Angeles, is home now to nine residents (six women, three men), aged sixty-five to eight-seven, who came together as strangers. The house was bought through a block grant from the U.S. Department of Housing and Urban Development via the City of Los Angeles Community Development Department. The city holds title to the house; ALA has a twenty-five-year lease. The residents are charged a monthly fee.

Another option is ECHO (Elder Cottage Housing Opportunities) housing, where you would live in a freestanding, removable cottage placed in the yard of a son or daughter's home. You could have your privacy and independence while remaining in your community. Unfortunately, ECHO housing is not readily available throughout the United States because of individual community zoning regulations.

Legal Advice

If you decide to buy or sell (condo, co-op, house), *please* consult a lawyer, specifically one who specializes in real estate law. Remember that the broker is out to make the deal, to earn a commission. The lawyer is for you, to put all the pieces together. The lawyer should review the contract, assess the property's value and determine whether it's a good buy and a wise investment, and, if it is, close on the purchase.

The lease you sign is a binding contract on both sides. Read every page and every clause. Understand and know what you are signing. (Are there clauses regarding cost-of-living increases? premature termination? pets? Can you abide by these regulations?)

You may be able to find a lawyer who will review your situation without charge. (Ask if there's a consultation fee.) You can get referrals from the local tenants and political organizations. Use *their* expertise to ensure your legal rights as tenant or owner.

Physical Move

Ready, set, go. It's emotionally and physically tough to move. Good planning can make things easier. Get all the help you can. Remember that when you get where you're going, it takes time to adjust. Everything doesn't have to be unpacked in the first twenty-four hours. A move is a major undertaking. Be gentle on yourself.

=====

One woman who thought she'd settled in for life is Rose Gale. She's a seventy-four-year-old widow, a childhood victim of polio, who today wears a heavy metal brace on her leg and walks with hand-held crutches. A small, sturdy woman with sparkling blue eyes, she moved in 1977, into a Manhattan retirement hotel where she rents a private room and bath. Satisfied with the location and accommodations, she believed it was her last move.

Then on November 7, 1983, during the lunch hour in the community dining room, the permanent nature of her housing was thrown into jeopardy. At that time, one of the owners of the building circulated through the room, informing the residents that the building was to be sold. Plans were in progress to create a condominium. The residents would face eviction in thirty days.

"There was pandemonium. I could feel my stomach turn over and my head begin to throb. People sat stunned or left the room in the middle of their meal. I'd always been an active person, speaking out, involved, an organizer. So people, on their way out, stopped and asked, 'What will we do now, Rose? What will we do?'

"I managed to get to my room and immediately got on the telephone. I think I was still in shock, but I knew I had to get help, to let someone know what was happening. I started with the congressional district office. They gave me additional numbers to call, including advocacy groups for the aging and tenants' organizations.

"On what seemed like little or no sleep, in the space of days, fifty-three community groups formed into a coalition to support our rights. All of a sudden I was a media star, appearing on TV and pleading our case in the papers.

"I had to try to save my home. I think I'd die if I had to move, to go someplace where I'd be isolated. This was *my* neighborhood. I'm comfortable. Everything is within reach. I'm near music, near the museums. Living here allows me to be on my own as a completely functional person. How could I give up my life?

"There were two hundred residents here. We're now down to forty-one. In the midst of all the publicity, people were being pressured to leave. They were taken to lunch and cajoled into other residences and homes. They were scared into moving, and I can't blame them.

"The fighting held me together. I used the stress and anxiety for positive action. I testified before city boards and commissions. We took the case to court. There were numerous hearings. Our lawyers, God bless them, worked for free. Finally, to make a long story short, the decision went in our favor. The issue boiled down to the fact we were rent-stabilized and therefore could not be evicted.

"I'm sure there'll be an appeal. At the moment we're in a holding pattern. Services have been curtailed. The air conditioning is off; the staff has been cut; the quality of the food has deteriorated. But we're holding on!

"What they tried to do to us was cruel and inhuman. They operated from greed. They didn't consider the rights or needs of the older people who'd chosen to live here.

"I had to fight. This is my home and my life!"

For More Information

Organizations

Apartment Sharing
The Jewish Council for the Aging
6111 Montrose Road
Rockville, MD 20852

Weinfield Group Living Residence
1 S. Franklin Street
Chicago, IL 60606

Share-A-Home, Inc.
1950 Lee Road
Winter Park, FL 32789

Project Match
277 W. Hedding St.
San Jose, CA 95110

Publications

The National Directory on Housing for Older People. Request from National Council on the Aging, 600 Maryland Avenue, SW, Washington, DC 20024.

Housing Choices for Older Homeowners and *Housing Options for Older Americans*. These are free. Send to AARP, 1909 K Street, NW, Washington, DC 20049.

Questions About Condominiums. Available from U.S. Department of Housing and Urban Development, Publications Division, Washington, DC 20410.

Books

Michaels, Joseph. *Prime of Your Life.* Boston: Little, Brown & Co., 1983.

Musson, Noverre. *National Directory of Retirement Residences: Best Places to Live When You Retire.* New York: Frederick Fell Pubs., 1982.

Salwen, Judy. *Solo Retirement.* New York: Dodd, Mead & Co., 1983.

Sumichrast, Michael, Ronald G. Shafer, and Marika Sumichrast. *Planning Your Retirement Housing.* Washington, D.C.: AARP; Glenview, Ill.: Scott, Foresman & Co., 1984. (An AARP Book)

12

Leisure Time

One ought every day to hear a little music, read a good poem, see a fine picture, and, if possible, speak a few reasonable words.

—Johann Wolfgang von Goethe

Perhaps you've never given a thought to the idea of leisure time. There was a job, a family, and the house. But what happens when the job is over, the family dispersed, and the house—well, it doesn't really need twenty-four-hour care. So let's say you're sitting around, in a perfectly spotless environment, wondering what to do with yourself.

Is there an interest you never had time to pursue? something you once said you'd love to try? an activity you're longing to do? a place you'd like to see?

Do you want to sit and dream? watch the soaps? read the classics? learn to type? play the flute? plant a garden? collect miniatures? take driving lessons? support a local candidate? go back to school? join a bridge club? Do you have a story to write or a song to sing? a desire to take up acting? Would working in clay, or oils or fabric, put a sparkle in your eyes?

Now is the time to listen to your inner voice. Now is the time to acknowledge your wishes, dreams, and fantasies. Now is the time to swallow that lump (believe me, I've felt it many times), take a deep breath, and jump!

Adjustment to Leisure

Some women revel in their newfound leisure time. The day after Sara retired, she put on her nightgown for a week. There was nothing physically wrong. "I'd always been so dependable—a perfect attendance record, never late, never coddled myself. For the first five working days," she told me, "after the going-away party, I luxuriated in bed. No alarm clock going off. No ten-minute coffee break. No lunch counter sandwich. I snacked when I wanted, made some gorgeous meals, and just plain indulged myself. It was an at-home vacation I felt I deserved. And after this pampering break I was ready to embark on this new phase of my life, intending to enjoy it to the hilt."

Some women are at a loss. Beth was one. A former elementary school principal who had lived by schedules and lists with never enough time, she suddenly found herself unable to cope with endless days and nothing to do. By eight o'clock she'd had breakfast, was dressed and ready, yet had nowhere to go. Leisure time for her was a source of irritation.

"After seven weeks of fits and starts, I finally found a plan that worked for me." And it was?

"I work three days a week at a day-care center. They pay a nominal fee for my expertise. And it's terrific for me to be back with the kids.

"On the fourth day I volunteer my services at an adult home. Since I've always made my own clothes, I'm a natural to teach sewing and dressmaking. I also run a group on fashion trends and styles.

"The fifth day is just for me. I force myself to stay in bed, even if I'm not sleepy, till at least nine. Then I take a Spanish lesson at the local Y, go for a swim, take a sauna, and get my hair done. I might visit friends in the afternoon or go to a movie or a museum.

"The most difficult thing was learning not to feel guilty about having free time, to understand and accept that I could be nice to me. It has taken serious work, a conscious effort to make myself relax and slow down."

Reading and Word Power

Books have always been a source of joy for me. Through them I've rediscovered the past, thought about the present, and explored the future. I read for various reasons, depending on my needs. I read for romance, adventure, and escape.

If you've never tried reading aloud, try it. You're probably saying, "Oh, no. I'd feel foolish." Don't. Instead, concentrate on hearing the words. Experience the drama, the emotion, the feelings.

Memorize your favorite poems. Over the years I've enjoyed such diverse poets as Nikki Giovanni, Ogden Nash, e.e. cummings, Erica Jong, Robert Lowell, and Judith Viorst.

Gain inspiration from quotations. On the bulletin board above my desk, I have fourteen quotes. Some offer comfort; some make me laugh; some give me courage. All have meaning to my life.

And all these words are free for the taking. I urge you to visit your local library. If you don't have a library card, make it your business to obtain one. *This* month! What does your library offer? Aside from books, can you borrow records, filmstrips, and slides? Does it have special activities? Are there discussion groups? afternoon lectures? poetry readings? If not, why not?

Rona, a woman who considers the library her second home, volunteers one morning a week to read to preschool children. The activity gives the mothers a much-needed break, the children are enthralled, and Rona gets to share her love of words with a new generation of readers.

How can reading become a social event? A group of

women in Lauderhill, Florida, recycle their paperbacks every other Saturday. They socialize over coffee and cake and then exchange their just-read novels and detective stories. Each woman purchases one paperback a month to keep up the flow of new contributions.

Another group of women, in Westport, Connecticut, meet on a monthly basis. They divide up the best-seller list, obtain the books (by direct purchase or through the library), and prepare a short report (plot summary, style, information about author, recommendation) to present to the others.

And another group, this one in Baltimore, Maryland, was formed through a common love of poetry. After a potluck dinner, the six women read and discuss their favorite poems.

Poetry

You *too* can write a poem. Oh yes you can! Take a blank piece of paper. Put the name of a friend or relative at the top. Now describe that person so we can see him or her, so we'd recognize the person if he or she walked through the door. For example:

> Susie
> five-year-old granddaughter
> brown flyaway braids
> quick to laughter and tears
> scabs on knees and elbows
> waiting for the tooth fairy

Don't worry about spelling or punctuation. Don't worry about a rhyme, unless it comes naturally. Just present a picture.

Take another piece of paper. Put the name of a color at the top. What does it remind you of? How does the color make you feel?

What words do you associate with loneliness? celebration? age? vacation? pet? Write a poem describing each concept. Think up some others.

Diaries and Journals

More words. Your own. Did you ever keep a diary? Did you ever note what you wore? the treachery of a best friend? the injustice of a teacher? Today more and more women are keeping journals. The difference between the diary and the journal is that in the journal you not only note the event, but you also record your feelings. Your journal is a place for dreams and fantasies—for conversations with yourself, for thoughts you'd never speak out loud. It's the place to sort out problems and clarify issues.

Word Study

And there's another way to use word power. A friend of mine reads the dictionary and makes flash cards of interesting words. (She writes the word and definition on a 3″ × 5″ card.) She packs them in a plastic sandwich bag and pops them into her purse. Whenever she finds herself waiting—in a bank line, in the doctor's office—she reviews her words. She is never bored, her vocabulary has improved, and she is a whiz at crossword puzzles!

The more you read, the more you play with words and ideas, the more you stretch your reality and imagination. What could be bad about that?

Oral Histories

You haven't thought about an incident in years. The trigger could be a photograph, a phrase, or a meeting with a friend you haven't seen in a long time. These are the moments when you reflect on the past. Perhaps you smile as you remember your achievements or tear up over recalled mistakes and failures.

How can you save what was? How can you hang on to the memories, both good and bad? Through a method known as oral history, you can record what your life was like. An oral history is the tape recording of a person's reminiscences of certain events.

It can be a way to preserve the past. It allows you to

share a period of time with others who may not have been with you. You can tape yourself and give the tape as a gift to your children or grandchildren, discuss it with friends, or save it only for yourself.

The price of a tape recorder has dropped dramatically due to the abundance of recorders now flooding the market. You can even find an inexpensive one at your discount drugstore.

If you are hesitant about where to begin, start with your childhood and work chronologically up to the present.

Life Review

Another way of recording and looking at your life is through the life review. Maggie Kuhn, the well-known leader of the Gray Panthers, explained how it works:

"The life review process gives people a sense of their own history. By reviewing the past, a person gains courage, strength, and hope to deal with the future.

"You begin by drawing a life line. The area above the line is for your private life, your personal existence; those close to you are a part of that. Then below you write in the powerful conditions, the influences of society. All of us are shaped by both the private and the public factors.

"The beginning of the process is to look at the year of your birth. What was the situation in your family at that time? In society? The closure date is when you feel you may die. That's shocking for some people to even contemplate.

"By looking back at the crises of your life, you see that you've survived those. Why should you think you won't survive what you are going through now? The life review gives you strength and the feeling that you can cope. Look at all the things you did, all the changes, all the disappointments that you've been through—and survived.

"The life review shows what you have done and where you have been and lets you think about where you want to go. It's a process of continuous change and growth."

Life reviewing and reminiscence can be therapeutic tools to retrieve memories of the past in order to come to terms with the future.

Hobbies

A hobby is an activity you engage in for pleasure. You might do it outdoors (like gardening) or restrict it to a tabletop (like collecting interesting stamps). ("I keep my stamp books open on a bridge table in the den. They're ready whenever I am." Edith, sixty-four.)

It is a good idea to have a number of hobbies at the same time. If you get stuck on one or become bored or tired, you can go on to one of the others.

Nelda, seventy-four, whose hobbies for the last three years include making dollhouse furniture and hooking rugs, spends part of each day on both.

In choosing a hobby, find something that will be satisfying—that will give you a feeling of success. Charlotte began doing needlepoint two years ago. "It's portable, so I can always take it with me. When my fingers are busy, I don't think about shoveling food into my mouth. Most of all, when I look at my needle-point pillows or the designs I've framed, I feel an enormous sense of pride."

Collecting is a fast-growing hobby for many women. Lee, sixty, collects cup and saucer sets. Because she loves flowers, that's one criterion for selection. Another is the shape of the cup's handle; the more unusual, the better. Her friends know of her interest and scout for additions when they are away.

Some collections start by chance. Donna, seventy, known for the special cookies she bakes, started saving all kinds of containers for packing purposes. She began to collect antique tins, then realized it was becoming harder and harder to part with them. "The designs were intricate, the colors soothing, the shapes different. Instead of hiding them in a closet to use for packing, I put them out where I could enjoy their variety. Soon I was hooked. The cookies now go out in aluminum foil!"

Popular collectibles include thimbles, pillboxes, teaspoons, paper fans, a specific stuffed animal (for example, teddy bears or frogs), candles, mugs, state memorabilia, and paperweights.

You can also collect things that are absolutely free. Women save matchbook covers, menus, restaurant place mats, beach shells, stones, postcards and stamps from vacationing friends, autographed pictures (write to your favorite movie star), and memorable quotes.

Take a look around. You might be a collector without even knowing it!

Remember that when you are looking for a new hobby, try to find one you can share with others. It's great when you find something you love to do. But work in total isolation can also be a cop-out if there is nothing else in your life. Is there a publication or trade bulletin to which you can subscribe? where you can exchange information? where you can perhaps find a pen pal? Can you take a class to further your skill? Is a conference being held where you can meet others who share your interest?

Whether your hobby is a passing fad, a lifelong passion, or just pleasant recreation, the choice and intensity of interest is up to you.

Volunteer Work

In the last few years there has been considerable discussion on volunteerism. Some say women should be paid for what they do, that volunteers take away jobs from paid workers. Some volunteers view their activities, their donation of time to a good cause, as its own reward.

The Peace Corps had Lillian Carter. And Ethel Merman donated her time (over ten years) to Roosevelt Hospital in New York City.

Some volunteer programs receive government funding. Others, local in origin, may provide travel expenses to and from the work place.

ACTION is the umbrella government agency that sponsors numerous volunteer positions for pay. One example is the Foster Grandparent Program.

Foster grandparents are parent substitutes for children who lack normal relationships with parents or grandparents. The program helps children who are in pediatric wards of hospitals; in homes for the dependent and neglected; and in institutions for the mentally retarded, emotionally disturbed, or physically handicapped.

In this program, age works in your favor. Volunteers must be at least sixty years old, in good health, and have a low income. If you are approved as a volunteer, there is a forty-hour orientation and training session. Benefits include a modest stipend, hot meals, and carfare.

For information on this and other ACTION programs, call the toll-free telephone number 800-424-8580.

At various times in my life I've been a rape victim advocate, an aide in a mental hospital, and a tutor to elementary school children and have answered a hot line at a suicide prevention center. All were volunteer jobs performed without pay. The common threads were that I enjoyed helping people and wanted to give back to my community. In the bargain I felt useful and worthwhile.

A volunteer job can fill empty hours and get you out of the house. It is an opportunity to take your attention off yourself and place it on someone or something else. It can be a chance to learn new skills and new ways of interacting. It can be a way of expanding your social network. It can be a new form of identity.

A woman I know spends her Thanksgiving at a shelter for battered women. She helps prepare and serve the dinner. Another woman works two hours a week teaching English to a foreign student. And a third gives hours too numerous to count to coordinate three benefits a year for her favorite charity. It doesn't matter *what* you do or how often you do it. What does matter is that when you make your time commitment, you keep it.

"It seems women have always done volunteer work," said Chris Filner, director of the Women's Center at the YWCA in New York City. "Schools, politics, and society need volunteers to function effectively. For most women it can be a productive and satisfying experience. But it's important that women are not taken advantage of. They need to be aware of their needs. They need to balance what they're giving with what they're getting."

One further note. Volunteer work is something you *choose* to do. If there ever comes a time when you feel exploited, speak up. If you don't feel that there has been a resolution of the problem, leave.

Before you decide on volunteer work, consider these questions.

☐ How much time do you want to give (for example, one morning, two days, or one evening a week)?

☐ Do you want to work with people or animals or do paperwork?

☐ How important is financial compensation?

☐ Do you want to do something completely new, or would you be more comfortable using familiar skills?

You can locate sources of volunteer work through religious organizations, civic and social service bulletins, newspapers, the local library, schools, hospitals, community centers, the local chapter of the National Organization for Women, the Urban League, and your city's Department of Aging.

Travel

One year after my husband died, I went to Mexico City and Acapulco for a ten-day vacation. I was back home in a week.

What went wrong? Everything, as far as I was concerned.

I had no planned itinerary. I hadn't done my homework in regard to where I was going and what I wanted to see.

I didn't realize the custom of dining late, so on the first night I felt like a child with my face pressed against the locked doors of the dining room, starving.

I hadn't confirmed my reservation from Mexico City to Acapulco. I lost the booking, then sat in the airport for six hours waiting for another flight.

In Acapulco I shared my out-of-the-way hotel room with numerous salamanders—for four hours. It took that long to realize I didn't have to stay in what for me was a totally untenable situation.

In Mexico City my tiny hotel was populated by foreigners. I was the only American, the only one who spoke English. In Acapulco the new hotel I picked out of the phone book turned out to be a honeymoon haven.

And although I daily *forced* myself to sign up for bus tours, in both cities, and *tried* to connect with people, in the evenings I was alone and lonely. (Lonely was standing on my terrace at sunset, overlooking the crowd on the patio below dancing to the beat of the mariachis. I wanted to cry and did.)

Many successful vacations and many, many miles later, I no longer shudder when I look back on that maiden trip. The lesson, first time out, was clear. The next time I traveled alone I would be prepared.

The first step is to choose a travel agent. (Ask friends for recommendations. Or look one up in your telephone book.) What can the agent do that you can't? She, or he, can save you time by helping you find the trip that is tailored to *your* interests, abilities, and budget. The agent can order your plane tickets; advise on tours; book cars, hotels, and sight-seeing trips; help with visas and passport; and even give you the weather report on your planned arrival.

And her services are free! Travel agents make their commissions from the airlines, hotels, and tour operators they use for your bookings.

There are an estimated twenty-two thousand travel agents nationwide. How do you choose?

One of the keys to finding good professional service is experience. It's important that your travel agent has it. Where has the agent been? What has she (or he) enjoyed seeing and doing? Does the agent have feedback from single women your age?

Will the agent answer your questions? Does she have numerous suggestions for trips in your price range? Does she have time for you even if your trip is a small one? Does she understand your needs?

What does her agency look like? Is the staff professional? interested? friendly? Is there a variety of up-to-date free brochures? What is the policy on trip cancellation? How long has the agency been in business? (Check out its reputation with your local Better Business Bureau.) Is your agent a member of the national American Society of Travel Agents (ASTA)?

You could go to a tennis camp, sail on a freighter, attend summer school at a foreign university, tour the great museums and concert halls, go backpacking in Hawaii, or even go to a hotel in your own city!

You can leave your home and return (by choosing the right trip) thinner, smarter, more serene, more cultured, able to play a musical instrument or speak a foreign language—and even as a nonsmoker.

Before you decide on a vacation, do these things.
- Browse through travel folders and guides.
- Talk to friends who have traveled. (What was their best vacation? Why?)
- Think about your own needs. Do you want adventure? romance? information? a complete rest?
- Consider whether you want to be on your own or would be more comfortable traveling with a group.
- Consider whether you can share a room with a stranger or feel that your privacy is worth the extra money.
- Figure out how much you have to spend.

Before you go on any trip, do the following:
- See your travel agent.
- Choose the trip that is exactly right for you.
- Find out as much about the place as you can.
- Get the necessary papers and pretrip medical care.
- Buy traveler's checks and obtain foreign currency if necessary.
- Make certain you have confirmations and vouchers.
- Get suggestions on tipping.
- Plan luggage and packing needs.
- Tell relatives and friends of your plans and give out your itinerary.
- Get a haircut.
- Stop your mail and newspaper service.

Before you pack for a trip, consider the following:
- Take half of what you planned on taking.
- Use only one suitcase and a small overnight bag.
- Color-coordinate all separates and use layers for varied weather conditions.
- Pack a folding umbrella.
- Pack items in separate plastic bags (for example, blouses, sweaters, bras, stockings) so there'll be less wrinkling and you'll be able to find things more easily. Include extra bags for dirty laundry and purchases.

□ Take an alarm clock, any special medicines, additional prescriptions, and extra eyeglasses.

□ Make a list of all the items you pack. Tape it to the inside cover of your suitcase. Check it each time you change your room.

A word of caution on travel safety: when you locked the door to your home, remember that you didn't leave behind your common sense. Use your own good judgment. If you're uncertain of local customs, check with the desk clerk or concierge.

Don't flash jewelry or wads of cash.

If you're on a tour and decide to go off on your own, let someone know your destination.

In the hotel, take time to note the safety precautions. What should you do in case of fire? Where are the exits located? How can you summon a doctor if you become ill?

Don't leave valuables or cash on display in your room.

Use the same precautions in taking care of yourself on a trip that you would at home. (Come on, would you really walk along a deserted beach at four in the morning?)

One of the safest ways to have cash on hand while abroad is traveler's checks. If you lose them, you can recover the full value with proof you are the purchaser. Veteran travelers will tell you to leave a photocopy of the receipt, as well as the serial numbers of the checks, with someone back home. Also place the checks and receipts in different places. Always make sure the issuing organization has offices in the vicinity of your journey. It's also wise to carry at least twenty dollars in cash in the currency of your destination country for use upon arrival for luggage porters, taxi drivers, and emergency phone calls.

If you become ill while abroad, call the hotel desk and have them summon a doctor. Or, before you go, you can obtain a free directory of English-speaking doctors around the world by writing to IAMAT (International Association for Medical Assistance to Travelers), 736 Center Street, Lewiston, New York 14092.

How Other Women Handle Traveling

☐ "I make a 'to do' list and bring along whatever I need to accomplish the chores—balancing my checkbook, catching up on correspondence, or doing reading I never had a chance to do."

☐ "I always study some of the language of the place I'm visiting so I can get more of the local color and flavor."

☐ "On an airplane, I ask for an aisle seat. You have the freedom to look to the left or right and even get to a stewardess for assistance in moving once the aircraft is in flight."

☐ "I try to go on a group tour so that all luggage and arrangements are handled with a minimum of trouble."

☐ "I take a private room, since I don't want to share with a stranger. There's enough 'people time' for me during the day and evening."

☐ "I try to find out from my travel agent if anyone in my area is going on the tour, and then I call to get acquainted."

☐ "On all forms of transportation, I carry a small throw pillow for naps."

☐ "Early on I try to make an impression on the stewardess, purser, conductor, or chauffeur so the person will remember me. I find that some conversation or being a bit more patient than my fellow travelers establishes a rapport that usually brings me special attention, favors, and even invitations for socializing."

☐ "Prior to the trip I check with all the people I know to see if *they* know anyone I could look up at my destination. It's always easier to tour a new area with a local."

- "I dress according to the type of people I'm interested in attracting."
- "I take lots of cash."
- "I speak up. I don't wait around *hoping* to be helped."
- "I've learned that it's always wise to wait before getting too friendly with a stranger on a trip. Then you won't feel trapped if you decide you really don't like the other person."
- "When I arrive, I check the schedule of the local universities and museums for evening lectures or events. It's safe and fun."
- "I ask lots of questions so as to meet people and get a feel for the place I'm visiting."
- "I make eye contact to let people know I'm in control."
- "Although I'm not religious, I try to attend services. I've done this in over half a dozen new cities, and people have been overwhelmingly kind and considerate—even inviting me home for dinner!"
- "I always take along some pictures of family and friends to prop on my bureau. Looking at familiar faces gives me courage to be more adventurous."
- "I clean my house from top to bottom *before* I leave. After a vacation that might be more work than rest and a long flight home, all I want to do is take a long, sudsy bath and flop down between clean sheets."
- "I keep back the fear of traveling alone by reminding myself that *he* always complained—about the bed, the food, the sight-seeing, the constant clicking of my camera."
- "If I decide to travel with a friend, I make sure we agree on the ground rules. Are we compatible in terms of what we want out of the trip? Do our habits mesh—I like to sleep late, does she? What happens if I meet someone and she doesn't—can we talk openly about jealousy and hurt feelings? Do we

have a comparable amount of money to spend? This may sound harsh, but I'd rather work these things out in my *own* living room than in the middle of a hotel lobby in some strange country!"

□ "I travel off-season. It's less expensive, and the sights I want to see aren't crowded with tourists."

□ "This is corny, but I try to remember to 'whistle a happy tune.' I'm prepared for periods of loneliness and for snafus like missed connections, poor service, and bad weather. When you're traveling, it pays to be tolerant and to have a sense of humor."

□ "It becomes almost too easy to opt for room service after a busy day. Sometimes I give in to the desire. More often I talk myself down to the dining room, thinking there'll be plenty of time to rest and eat alone when I get home."

□ "I've never been comfortable using a camera. Instead, wherever I travel, I buy postcards and note my feeling state, my impressions, and the date on the back of each."

Remember, when you travel, it's on *your* time and money. Take advantage of both by good planning.

For More Information

Organizations

Volunteer Talent Bank
AARP
1909 K Street NW
Washington, DC 20049
(Uses computers to match potential volunteers with suitable volunteer positions.)

Publications

On Travel

Facts and Advice for Airline Passengers, Aviation Consumer Action Project, PO Box 19029, Washington, DC 20036.

Publications (continued)

On Hobbies

American Craft
American Craft Council
Publishers
22 West 55th Street
New York, NY 10019

Needle and Thread
Happy Hands Publishing
4949 Byers
Ft. Worth, TX 76107

Creative Crafts
Carsten's Publications, Inc.
Box 700
Newton, NJ 07860

Nutshell News
Boynton and Associates
Clifton House
Clifton, VA 22024

Books

Baldwin, Christina. *One to One: Self-Understanding Through Journal Writing.* New York: M. Evans & Co., 1977.

Bartlett, John. *A Collection of Familiar Quotations.* New York: Philosophical Library, 1965.

Kaminsky, Marc. *The Uses of Reminiscence.* New York: Haworth Press, 1984.

Massow, Rosalind. *Travel Easy: The Practical Guide for People Over 50.* Washington, D.C.: AARP; Glenview, Ill.: Scott, Foresman & Co., 1985. (An AARP Book)

Partnow, Elaine, ed. *The Quotable Woman.* New York: Doubleday & Co., 1978.

Progoff, Ira. *At a Journal Workshop.* New York: Dialogue House Library, 1975.

Sarton, May. *Journal of a Solitude.* New York: W. W. Norton & Co., 1977.

Zimmerman, William. *How to Tape Instant Oral Biographies.* New York: Guarionex Press, 1979.

13

Your Sexual Self

Quite a few women told me that they thought it was sex, not youth, that's wasted on the young.

—Janet Harris

Women are often reluctant to talk about sex, even to one another. Perhaps it's because many of us grew up hearing it was dirty, sinful, and bad. Discussed in whispers, information was sketchy and terse.

During the last decade, along with a new spirit of celebration regarding the achievements and strides made by women, we have also seen a new openness in the area of sexual life. Women are being presented with information and choices that, at times, are confusing. No one—I repeat, *no one*—has to do anything that makes her uncomfortable or causes her embarrassment. But having the choices to consider, to accept or reject according to one's background and wishes, is, I think, a woman's right.

If you're newly single, being alone now can be unsettling. You can feel sexually unlovable, especially as your body changes with age. Media exposure of the "perfect" female body has not helped our perceptions. Honestly, among the women you know, how many have model-type figures? It seems the concentration on what you *should* look like rather than on what you *do* look like contributes to a cycle of unrealistic expectations.

If you've come to accept your self, it's time to extend that same warm gesture to your body. Maybe you're flat-chested, hippy, or bottom-heavy. So? Some features you can change through diet, posture, and exercise. Those you can't, you need to learn to accept.

In addition to examining attitudes regarding your body, what are your attitudes about your sexual self? Can you think back to the sexual messages you received while growing up? Do they fit you now? There are ways to assess your sexual feelings as an aid to considering options for the future: (1) You might choose a close friend and compare sexual histories. Discuss parental injunctions and peer comments. What was the social and moral tenor of your community while growing up? (2) You could reconstruct your own social and sexual history on paper. Who was your first boyfriend? Describe your first date, first parties, and first kiss. (3) You can read a number of popular books out today on women and sex (see the list at the end of this chapter). Compare your history and attitude with what you are reading. You might follow one of the exercise programs some books offer to develop your sexual potential (see Barbach, *For Yourself*). (4) You could call a women's center or college for a list of discussion groups or lectures on sexuality.

Sexual Desire

Older women have often been stereotyped as being sexless. Recent data reveal findings to the contrary. In a survey of eight hundred American men and women conducted by Drs. Bernard Starr and Marcella Weiner, 87 percent of the female respondents said that sex after menopause was the same or better. The majority said they were sexually active. In the same study, a majority felt that there was nothing wrong with masturbation.

What about menopause and sexual desire? *Menopause* is a term used to describe the end of the menstrual years. Menopause is a cutoff point to reproductive life, but it does not mark the end to sexual response. As indicated in the Starr-Weiner study, many women experience a renewal of sexual interest and enjoyment. In fact, sexual activity can be a psychological boost for women feeling vulnerable because of bodily changes.

The shibboleths and superstitions regarding menopause are legion. But not all women react in the same way, nor do they all undergo similar symptoms. According to the Sex Information and Education Council of the U.S., not more than 10 to 15 percent of women going through menopause seek medical help. If *you* are experiencing physical or psychological discomfort, you can restore your sense of control by talking to your physician or gynecologist. Be sure the doctor you have is someone you feel comfortable with in discussing intimate sexual changes and feelings, and if you're not satisfied with your present doctor, seek another who is more open to such discussions.

One of the forms of treatment to consider during difficult menopausal years is hormone replacement therapy. The pros and cons of this therapy are widely debated. Estrogen has been found to reduce many of the symptoms of menopause. But it does not stop the aging process. It may, in fact, be a cause of uterine cancer. In many cases, estrogen is prescribed in combination with progesterone, another female sex hormone. There are both definite benefits, such as bone strengthening, and risks to this currently controversial treatment.

Masturbation

Masturbation, sexual self-pleasuring with or without a vibrator, is to many older women taboo. JoAnne DenBeste, a sex educator and counselor in Portland, Oregon, when asked if masturbation could be considered harmful, replied this way: "Only if it's against your value system. And this is an individual decision. You need to ask yourself if this is appropriate and responsible behavior for you."

Masturbation can be just one expression of your sexuality. It's a way of acknowledging, exploring, and satisfying your sexual feelings. A secondary gain is that by learning what pleases you, you become more confident about sex when you are with a partner.

Orgasm

Those pioneering experts of sexual research and education, Masters and Johnson, in *Human Sexual Response*, stated, "The aging human female is fully capable of sexual performance at orgasmic response levels, particularly if she is exposed to regularity of effective sexual stimulation. In short, there is no time limit drawn by advancing years to female sexuality."

According to Dr. Wardell Pomeroy, a colleague of sex researcher Alfred Kinsey, "Granted good health, aged women can have orgasms or multiple orgasms as well as they did in their forties and fifties, which is their peak."

Some women report being orgasmic only through intercourse or oral sex. Others experience orgasm through manual stimulation of the clitoris.

Closeness

Numerous women confided to me that it was not orgasm or the act of intercourse they missed but the closeness between two people. It may be holding each other in bed, kissing, cuddling, or touching. It can be massages and back rubs. It can be holding hands, a caress on the cheek, or a stroke of the arm. It can be inexplicable tenderness and caring between two friends. The longing, therefore, may not be for sex per se, but for human bonding.

Older Women/Younger Men

For women who choose *not* to be celibate—that is, to *have* sex—there's a new pairing to be considered, that of older women with younger men. For a widow who lost her husband to a heart attack, there can be a real fear of developing a relationship with a man of similar age who may also become ill. Ann Landers has said, "With women outliving men from four to six years, it makes sense to marry a younger man." I'd add that it makes perfect sense to date and be friends with them also. Why? Why not?

Having a younger friend, date, or lover may be good for your ego and for your looks. Beverly, sixty-five, talks about Jim, forty-nine: "I think male company is important to a woman at any age. I'm more aware now of how I look and of how I dress. I'm pampering myself with creams and oils—something I never did before. I want to be attractive to him. I want him to feel proud of me when we go out together. Jim is friend and lover, and I'm grateful we've found each other."

Some women are turning to younger men out of choice. The women's movement has urged them to try new things—to be creative, to open up their options. Some are no longer waiting to be chosen. They are doing the choosing.

Some women are turning to younger men out of necessity. Two out of three women will experience widowhood in their lifetime. And for every five formerly married women, there are three formerly married men. The number of social partners is on the decrease as older women see their male age peers turn to younger women.

In terms of sexual fulfillment, if an older man can be sexually reawakened by a younger woman, why can't the same hold true for an older woman and a younger man?

Some women complain about same-age or older men set in traditional role patterns—that they are not open to new thoughts or ideas, that sex is predictable.

These women say that with younger men there is a curiosity about life and people. There is the ability to see things from a new perspective and an attitude toward sex that is playful rather than forced.

In sexual relationships, it is important to look beyond the chronological age and see the person underneath the years. Alvin Toffler, the author and futurist, called this "stage not age." What is important is complementary values and interests. What should count is the level of personal development, not the number of decades.

Since our society is age-biased against older women, one must realize that people will talk about such relationships. So what? Let them. If you've found a younger man who likes you and makes you feel good about yourself, accept that and enjoy him!

Celibacy

Some women choose to be celibate. Others have celibacy chosen for them because of lack of opportunity. Women who choose to be celibate talk of getting in touch with a higher consciousness. They often see their celibate periods as a chance to direct their sexual energies into other activities.

Dr. Rose Dobrof, director of the Hunter College Brookdale Center on Aging, notes that some women were *never* really interested or involved with sex. It just wasn't an important part of their lives. Now widowed or divorced, there's a sense of relief that sexual activity is over. If a woman was not strongly sexual at thirty, she probably won't be sexual at sixty. If sex was something to be "gotten over with," or viewed through socialization with distaste, a sex-free life may be perfectly comfortable.

Same-Sex Pairing

Another pairing involves women loving women. Most of us have grown up believing same-sex love is a major taboo. Then why are some women choosing this option? It may be due to a shortage of available men. There are women who have had heterosexual relationships in their earlier life, yet in later life they find that a woman can satisfy their needs for closeness and sexual fulfillment. There can be a companionship, intimacy, and sharing of mutual attitudes and feelings. "As long as I have Helen [forty-five]," said Bobbie, fifty-five, "I'm not lonely or afraid of my aging. In fact she's what keeps me young. Her vitality, her interests, and her passions are really contagious."

It is also true that age can bring independence and confidence. Some women may have been attracted to other women in the past, and those feelings that were pushed down by convention or denied through uncertainty can now be expressed and acted upon.

Sexual Choices

However you feel, pro or con, whatever you decide, you don't have to get caught up in what has been termed the sexual revolution. (It does, however, seem to be waning.) "I should go to dinner, and dessert is in my bed? On a first date?" Lorraine, sixty-four, questioned. "Well, that's not how I live my life. If I'm expected to pay for dinner, I'll do it in cash, not flesh."

The question of sex may come up sooner than it used to in a relationship. You don't have to feel pressured. You don't have to prove yourself. You can say *no*. It's your body, and you can be in control. You can say, for instance: "I'd really like to get to know you better." "I like you, but I need some more time." "I'm not ready to make that commitment." "I'd feel more comfortable if we waited." Or you can just say, "No."

If you find you are having continued problems dealing with your sexual self, you may want to seek help. Resources may include your own doctor, a women's clinic counselor, or a therapist specializing in women's concerns.

It's *your* body, *your* emotions, *your* life.

For More Information

Organizations

American Association of Sex Educators, Counselors, and Therapists
Suite 304
5010 Wisconsin Avenue, NW
Washington, DC 20016

Senior Action in a Gay Environment (SAGE)
208 West 13th Street
New York, NY 10011

Publications

Sexual Life in the Later Years (Study Guide No. 12). Published by Sex Information and Education Council of the U.S. (SIECUS), 1855 Broadway, New York, NY 10023.

Books

Barbach, Lonnie Garfield. *For Yourself: The Fulfillment of Female Sexuality*. New York: Doubleday & Co., 1975.

Cutler, Winnifred Berg, Celso-Ramon Garcia, M.D., and David A. Edwards. *Menopause: A Guide for Women and the Men Who Love Them.* New York: W. W. Norton & Co., 1983.

Heiman, Julia, Leslie LoPiccolo, and Joseph LoPiccolo. *Becoming Orgasmic: A Sexual Growth Program for Women.* Englewood Cliffs, N.J.: Prentice-Hall, 1977.

Kerr, Carmen. *Sex for Women.* New York: Grove Press, 1977.

Lauersen, Niels, M.D., and Steven Whitney. *It's Your Body: A Woman's Guide to Gynecology.* New York: Grosset & Dunlap, 1977.

Seaman, Barbara, and Gideon Seaman. *Women and the Crisis in Sex Hormones.* New York: Rawson, Wade Pubs., 1977.

Seskin, Jane, and Bette Ziegler. *Older Women/Younger Men.* New York: Doubleday & Co., 1979.

Starr, Bernard, and Marcella Weiner. *The Starr-Weiner Report on Sex and Sexuality in the Mature Years.* New York: McGraw-Hill Book Co., 1981.

14

Coping with Sundays—and Other Common Problems

The supply of time is a daily miracle. You wake up in the morning and lo! your purse is magically filled with twenty-four hours of the unmanufactured tissue of the universe of life. It is yours! The most precious of your possessions.

—Arnold Bennett

Many women function splendidly during the week, enjoy their Saturday, and then fall apart on Sunday. Why? Perhaps it is due to a traditional mind-set where you picture a family getting together to perform chores and run errands, a lazy kind of day filled with people, good cheer, and a large midday meal. "Not true for me," you say, shaking your head.

To combat the Sunday blues, you need to structure your time and note the hours when you begin to feel lonely or bored. What activities can you schedule? Do you have a solo project to complete, or do you want to share your time with other people? Do you need a quiet bedroom day, or would you prefer to be outside and active? Chart this Sunday and plan for the next.

	This Sunday	Next Sunday
8:00 A.M.	_____	_____
9:00 A.M.	_____	_____
10:00 A.M.	_____	_____
11:00 A.M.	_____	_____
12 NOON	_____	_____

	This Sunday	**Next Sunday**
1:00 P.M.	_____	_____
2:00 P.M.	_____	_____
3:00 P.M.	_____	_____
4:00 P.M.	_____	_____
5:00 P.M.	_____	_____
6:00 P.M.	_____	_____
7:00 P.M.	_____	_____
8:00 P.M.	_____	_____
9:00 P.M.	_____	_____
10:00 P.M.	_____	_____
11:00 P.M.	_____	_____
12:00 P.M.	_____	_____

Sleeping

Now that you've gotten through the day, how do you feel about your night? I'm talking sleep. The night my husband went into the hospital for the first time, I slept on *my* side of the bed, an arm around *his* pillow and the broom by the night table. I still remember being startled by the night sounds, the silence in the house disturbed by the clock ticking off time and the tree branches stroking the windowpanes. I recall getting up, broomstick in hand, to recheck the lock on the back door. Restless, tossing and turning, I woke early. Sleep had increased my sense of battle fatigue. It had not been restorative. Although that night was many years ago, the memory lingers.

Elizabeth Kenny, the Australian nurse also known as Sister Kenny, remarked, "O sleep, O gentle sleep, I thought gratefully. Nature's gentle nurse!" Sometimes it is, and sometimes it's not.

Nina, seventy-four, sleeps four hours a night. Pearl,

fifty-five, says she needs eight hours to feel herself. What about you? Are you having trouble getting to sleep?

More than twenty-five million Americans suffer from chronic insomnia, persistent difficulty in sleeping so that the individual is always tired, sleepy, and anxious.

Dr. Quentin R. Regestein, director of the Sleep Clinic at Peter Bent Brigham Hospital in Boston, noted in an interview that many cases of insomnia are related to "irregular times of going to bed and arising; night work; daytime naps; sedentary daytime routines; overuse of caffeine; and chronic abuse of tranquilizers, sleeping pills, or alcohol."

Whereas a newborn *needs* 18 hours of sleep to feel rested, an older person can feel refreshed on from 4½ to 6½ hours of sleep. This becomes increasingly evident after the age of fifty-five.

Sleep may be disturbed if you are feeling anxious, worried, or depressed. Some women, rather than deal with their problems, use sleep as a way to avoid them. If you talk out your worries during the day, you won't have to take them into your bed at night.

If you wake earlier than usual, on a consistent basis, get up. Your body may be giving you a message that you need less sleep than you think you do. Use the extra time you gain to begin a new book or project.

To help you sleep, consider these suggestions.

- Check with your doctor to rule out any connection between insomnia and physical ailments.
- Avoid caffeine-containing beverages (coffee, tea, colas) during the evening hours.
- If you must drink, have a glass of warm milk; amino acids in milk have a sedative effect.
- Regulate your room temperature—not too hot or too cold.
- Try different types and weights of blankets.

□ Wear loose, not binding, bedclothes.
□ Keep your room as dark as possible (dark window shades can be purchased at your local department store).
□ Read a boring book.
□ Take a warm bath.
□ Don't *try* to fall asleep—the concentration will keep you awake.
□ Try responding to soothing sounds such as the hum of a fan or a radio talk show.
□ Try some exercise at least an hour before going to bed (walk around your block, do some yoga).
□ Don't use alcohol or tranquilizers—they can be both physically and psychologically addictive.
□ In bed, find a comfortable position and lie as still as possible; resist the urge to move.
□ Slow your breathing. Take a deep breath, let it out slowly, and swallow comfortably—relax.
□ Focus on a soothing mental picture—a country scene, a lake, an empty beach.

Housework

Shirley Conran, a homemaking expert, found that full-time housewives spend an average of fifty-five hours a week on household chores, while working women spend about thirty. Why the difference? It could be size of house, rate of efficiency, or method of setting priorities for the tasks to be done. Time management means exactly what it says. When Berda complains, "I never have enough time," she needs to weigh how she is filling her hours with what she wants to accomplish.

Do away with some of the chores you hate. Some women find ironing relaxing. I don't. In fact I consider it a waste of my time—so much so that I haven't ironed anything in over ten years. I do, though, get a sense of satisfaction from washing my kitchen floor. (Each to her own pleasure!)

Organizing Your Time and Efforts

To organize and better manage your time, ask yourself what is truly important. Would you rather work with clay than clean the tub? Are you someone who can't sleep if there are dishes in the sink? Can you close the door on a messy room and sit quietly doing needlepoint? What can you live with? How much clutter and disorder can you tolerate? Can you put your hands on last year's tax return? the photos from your vacation? your enameled earrings? Who are you cleaning for, yourself or visitors? What chores can you give up or let go? No one has yet convinced me that it is more important to dust than watch a sunset.

For those of you who can't decide what to tackle first, Peg Bracken, author of *The I Hate to Housewife Book,* suggests writing your chores on slips of paper along with some pleasant activities (watch soap opera, read a novel) and putting them all in a shoe box. Periodically, then, you close your eyes, draw a slip, and do whatever it says.

Moving right along, let's consider lists. I love them! I love making the ordered columns, and I love crossing out the items, signifying completion. Lists make me feel that I have control over my life. I list things to do and people to call. I carry a small, lined notebook in my purse to catch stray thoughts and jot down reminders. Each evening I review the pages. In my kitchen I keep a pad by the toaster to record things to buy. When I use the last of the orange juice or run out of tomato sauce, that product goes right down on the list.

Organize. This also implies learning to throw things out. Come on, when was the last time you wore that sweater with the fur collar and pearl buttons? Do you intend to read that stack of magazines collecting dust in the corner? Do you think it's getting to be a fire hazard? What about the assortment of jars and containers under the sink? Will you really have enough leftovers to fill them all? Can you throw any of them out? Sort through your closets, cabinets, drawers, and desk. If you don't use it, lose it. Have a garage sale. Donate clothing, household appliances, and knick-knacks to a favorite charity and collect a tax deduction. Organize what is left. Use anything to bring order out of chaos. Experiment with garment bags, plastic boxes, cardboard chests, under-the-bed boxes, and file cabinets (they now come in colors!). Explore the housewares section of your local department store. And don't neglect the hardware shop for additional space-saving ideas.

To free up your hours, consider alternative plans of action. A highly organized woman I know keeps all her party supplies (cheese boards, knives, trays, toothpicks, plastic cups, and napkins) in the bottom closet in her kitchen. Because she continually replenishes her stock, everything is in place and ready to be set out in fifteen minutes. She uses fancy paper products to minimize her cleanup.

Another woman abhors wasted trips in her neighborhood. To prevent this from happening, she leaves the things to be taken care of during the week on the table in her entry hall. She'll leave mail to go out, the bag with shoes to be heeled, the bundle of laundry, and the books to be returned to the library. Out on her regular errands, she simply makes some additional stops. To help her plan her route, she lists the places she'll visit in order, so as not to retrace her steps. She carries this list in her coat pocket.

Management consultant Elaina Zucker suggests setting up a home office to organize and deal with your paperwork problems. You can use a system of file folders. (Keep them lined up in a cardboard carton from the supermarket.) Separate folders might include (1) important documents; (2) insurance papers; (3) guarantees, warrantees, and instruction booklets; (4) tax records; (5) paid bills; (6) useful articles; and

(7) entertainment ideas. Create any additional folders that have relevance to your life.

Another paper tip comes from Selma, seventy-one. "I buy greeting cards in quantity every few months. I'll select half a dozen cards for each occasion: birthday, anniversary, get well, friendship, and new house. I sort them into sandwich bags and keep them in a kitchen drawer. I like knowing I'm always prepared, that my cards will go out on the right dates. It never seemed fair that someone should be disappointed because I wasn't able to get to the card shop."

Consider the value you place on your time. Anita becomes nervous waiting for a bus. Fifteen or twenty minutes go by, and she is impatiently tapping her foot, anxious to get where she is going. Deciding her time is worth money, she now chooses to take a taxicab instead of waiting at the bus stop. Placed in the same situation, Naomi copes differently. "I figure bus stops are for waiting. That's built in. So now I'm prepared. During the week I clip stories and articles from the newspapers and magazines I read. I staple each set together and tuck them into my bag. Whenever and wherever I wait, I just pull out my reading material and get started."

Home Repairs

What action should you take regarding simple home repairs? Should you get involved or call for professional help?

Theresa took a course. "I'm going to live the rest of my life as a single person. I figured I should know what to do if something goes wrong. The course is given on Saturday mornings at my local high school. An unexpected bonus was meeting a widower who was also a student."

Sharon felt a different way. "I'll learn how to do, to be responsible for, other things. Making repairs isn't for me. If something breaks in my apartment, I go to the Yellow Pages and dial for help. This is not an area in which I choose to be competent."

Dealing with an unexpected crisis (the refrigerator goes on the blink, the toilet gets plugged up, or the basement floods) can be unsettling. Stay calm. If you can't fix the problem yourself, get outside help. If you already have a list of service people—television repair person, plumber, carpenter, painter, exterminator—call one. ("For a while I called the man down the hall whenever I had a problem." Helen made a face and continued. "Then he asked what I was planning to do in return for his help. When I suggested making dinner, he said that wasn't what he had in mind. From then on I called a professional.") If the problem is not an emergency, try to get a number of telephone estimates before you have a service call. You can also ask friends for the names of people they have used with satisfaction.

Whether it's do it yourself or using service persons, you'll learn how to manage.

Advocacy

Okay. Now that you are managing, how about going a step further—how about a little righteous anger on behalf of a good cause? I believe in advocacy. I think as citizens we have a duty to stand up and be counted. We have a duty to speak for or against issues, causes, and people that affect our lives. The author James Baldwin said, "Not everything that is faced can be changed; but nothing can be changed until it is faced." You can help bring about change by joining an organized group. Or you can sign petitions, write letters, or make telephone calls.

You can also advocate on your own behalf. You can stand up for yourself. Consider what happened to Rita. This incident took place a couple of months ago.

Rita thought the checkout woman at her local super-market had been extremely rude. Although she asked that her purchases not be rung up until she had unloaded her cart, the woman ignored her request. When Rita asked that her groceries be double-bagged, she was again ignored. Rita could feel her anger build as she headed for the door. Then she stopped, turned back, and sought the manager. "I decided I couldn't let this go unnoticed. It bothered me. Was the woman just rude to me, all older people, or people in general? If she was having a bad day, well, that wasn't my fault. As far as I was concerned, her attitude reflected on the store, and if the message they were sending out was rudeness, I'd take my business elsewhere. I explained all this to the manager, and he couldn't have been more charming and polite. He apologized and said he'd speak to the woman, and as I turned to leave, he handed me a box of cookies. 'A goodwill gift,' he said. I know it was a tiny, tiny victory, but I'd stood up for myself and felt terrific."

Standing up for yourself *does* feel terrific. You have the right to complain about defective products, poor workmanship, and rude service. You have the right to be treated with courtesy. You have the right to an explanation of charges on any bill, receipt, or state-ment. You have the right not to be taken advantage of. And if you are, you must speak out.

Assertive behavior (standing up for yourself) is neither actively aggressive nor threatening to the other person. It is a way of getting what you want by listen-ing to yourself and verbalizing those feelings so the other person is not hurt. Assertive statements are usu-ally referred to as "I statements." (I feel badly when you speak to me that way. I hear what you're saying, but this is the way I feel. I'm sorry that you're ill, but I still need your help on this project.)

Assertive behavior also involves eye contact, facial gestures, and body language. If you express your anger to someone while you're sprawled in a chair with a grin on your face, you can't expect to be taken seriously.

An effective way to practice assertive behavior is to role-play different situations with a friend. What would you say if (1) you are overcharged in a restaurant, (2) someone criticizes your work, or (3) your friend constantly makes demands on your free time?

Assertive behavior can take different forms. To make yourself heard on product complaints, you can write a letter to the national president of the company involved. (The *Thomas Register* lists manufacturers' names and addresses. This book can be found in your library.) The *Consumer's Resource Handbook* suggests covering the following points in your letter: (1) your name, address, and home and work phone numbers; (2) the product name with serial or model number; (3) the date and location of the purchase; (4) the history of the problem; and (5) a statement of the specific action you want. In addition, it suggests that you enclose copies (not originals) of all pertinent documents (warranty, canceled check, receipt, and so on).

If you do not receive satisfaction from your letter, you can contact your local consumer office. The next level would be the State Office for Consumer Affairs.

An additional way to handle complaints is to notify the nonprofit Better Business Bureau (a total of 150 offices throughout the United States). Policies regarding services differ according to the individual offices. They *can* give you general information on products or services, reliability reports, background information on local businesses and organizations, and records of companies' complaint-handling performances. Many of the BBBs accept written complaints and will contact a firm on your behalf.

"I sometimes wonder," said Beth with a sigh, "whether I do any good when I write my letters. But then I think I'd hate myself if I didn't take a stand against something I considered intolerable or unjust. I think it boils down to my own sense of personal integrity."

How else can you be heard? There are two other possibilities: You can write a letter to the editor of your local newspaper. You can phone a radio call-in show to express your views.

The important point is not how or where to express yourself. Rather, it's that you choose to make a decision to act, to stand up and be counted.

Sometimes your voice will say, "I don't want to. No!" And that's okay too. You have the right to make mistakes, the right *not* to be superwoman.

Rest and Relaxation

In addition to setting priorities, organizing schedules, and possibly advocating for yourself and others, plan on taking time for rest and relaxation. If it's difficult for you to allow yourself some fun, by all means write *Fun* in your date book. Then stick to your schedule!

Thirty Ways to Spend Thirty Days

1. Give yourself an hour of bubbles. Take a bubble bath or buy some bubble gum and blow.
2. Too much junk mail or not enough? To have your name removed from or added to mailing lists that belong to the Direct Mail/Marketing Association, contact DMMA, 6 East 43rd Street, New York, NY 10017—Att: Mail Preference Service.
3. Spray the hem of your skirt lining or slip with perfume.
4. Have your handwriting analyzed or your astrological chart read.
5. Take an empty jar. Each night empty your purse of change and add to the jar. Save for a month; then buy yourself a treat.

6. Write this affirmation on an index card and tape it to your bathroom mirror: *I am an attractive single woman. I like who I am and what I am.*

7. The first week of August is National Smile Week. That doesn't mean you have to wait till then to give away one of yours.

8. Send a Valentine's Day card to a friend in any month *but* February.

9. Swap a skill with a friend. For instance, "If you cut out the dress pattern, I'll sew it."

10. Get a facial. Ask for a makeup consultation and demonstration.

11. Is your passport up-to-date? Do you need a new one? You can apply at approximately 825 postal facilities nationwide. The passport fee may be paid in cash or by check or money order. Call your post office for further information.

12. Make a list of your strengths. List twenty-five things you can do. (I can type. I can arrange flowers. I can make hems.) Spend thirty minutes appreciating yourself.

13. Have a nice good scream.

14. Try setting your hair with beer or frothy egg whites.

15. According to Dr. Frederic C. McDuffie of the Arthritis Foundation, "Laughter stimulates the brain to produce endorphins, which are hormones that ease pain." As medicine, then, try to find something each day to make you laugh.

16. Stock up on canned foods (ravioli, soups, hash). The portions are manageable when you're hungry and don't want to run to the market.

17. Send to the Government Printing Office for any of over five hundred publications, the majority of which are free. Write U.S. Government Books, New Catalog, Government Printing Office, Washington, DC 20402.

18. Keep your cologne in the refrigerator for an anytime cool pick-me-up.

19. Do you sing around the house? make up the words to your songs? Send for the free booklet *How to Market Your Songs the Professional Way* from Method Songwriting, PO Box 842, Tarzana, CA 91356.
20. Spend one hour browsing in a bookstore.
21. Learn about wines. Attend a tasting. These are often given by liquor stores to encourage business. There is usually no charge. You can learn the specifics (countries, growers, and good years) from the following books: *The Pocket Guide to Wine* by Barbara Ensrud, *The Pocket Encyclopedia of California Wines* by Bob Thompson, and *The World Atlas of Wines* by Hugh Johnson.
22. Organize a neighborhood watch group or a tenants' association. Invite an officer from your local precinct to one of the meetings. Have the officer discuss crime prevention and safety tips.
23. Keep a joke book. Record all stories, riddles, and one-liners that make you laugh. Review your book before you attend your next party.
24. Need to cuddle but there's no one special around? Who says grown women can't own stuffed animals? Pshaw! Get yourself a teddy bear for those lonely minutes.
25. Attend the opera. Study the libretto before you go.
26. Need a gift but don't have time to shop? Give a magazine subscription. Wrap the current issue of your choice and insert your own gift card.
27. On May 1, 1933, Nellie Tayloe Ross became the first female director of the U.S. Mint. In her honor, spend some money. Give yourself a treat and buy something totally impractical.
28. Try a thirty-minute nap.
29. Have someone take your picture. Send copies to friends and relatives.
30. Invest in a sketchbook and some colored marking pens. Draw, doodle, write a letter, make a card, or copy a favorite quotation.

Ralph Waldo Emerson felt this way about time: "Finish every day and be done with it. You have done what you could; some blunders and absurdities crept in. Forget them as soon as you can. Tomorrow is a new day. You shall begin it well and serenely and with too high a spirit to be encumbered with your old nonsense."

For More Information

Toll-free Hotline

Consumer Product Safety Commission: 800-638-2772. Evaluates safety of products on sale to the public.

Publications

On Making It Through the Night by Judith Willis. Write HHS Publication NO. (FDA) 80-3095, Office of Public Affairs, 5600 Fishers Lane, Rockville, MD 20857.

Working Woman Guide to Time Management by Elaina Zucker. Working Woman Magazine, 342 Madison Avenue, New York, NY 10173.

Consumer's Resource Handbook. Available free from Handbook, Consumer Information Center, Pueblo, CO 81009.

Books

Winston, Stephanie. *Getting Organized.* New York: Warner Books, 1978.

A Commencement Note

If you have never allowed yourself to be uncomfortable, you will never appreciate the warmth of comfort. If you don't take a risk, you'll stand rooted to the spot while others move around you. If you never jump into the waters, you'll never know how high you can hold your head. If you don't dream, you won't hope. If you never take charge, you'll be unsure of your power. And if you don't believe in yourself, who will believe in you and celebrate your specialness?

Alone—Not Lonely. We are all basically alone. How much we connect to others is up to us. How we live our lives is our decision. How we use our selves is our gift. Life goes on, and so must we.

For Further Reading

Books by, for, and about older women:

Butler, Robert N., M.D. *Why Survive? Being Old in America.* New York: Harper & Row, Pubs., 1975.

------, with Myrna Lewis. *Sex After Sixty: A Guide for Men and Women in Their Later Years.* New York: Harper & Row, Pubs., 1976.

Comfort, Alex, M.D. *A Good Age.* New York: Simon & Schuster, 1976.

Curtin, Sharon R. *Nobody Ever Died of Old Age.* Boston: Little, Brown & Co., 1972.

Gold, Don. *Until the Singing Stops.* New York: Holt, Rinehart & Winston, 1979.

Gordon, Ruth. *My Side.* New York: Harper & Row, Pubs., 1976.

Kanin, Garson. *It Takes a Long Time to Become Young.* New York: Doubleday & Co., 1978.

Kuhn, Maggie. *On Aging: A Dialogue.* Edited by Dieter Hessel. Philadelphia: Westminster Press, 1977.

LeShan, Eda. *On Living Your Life.* New York: Harper & Row, Pubs., 1982.

Robey, Harriet. *There's a Dance in the Old Dame Yet.* Boston: Little, Brown & Co., 1982.

Rubin, Lillian B. *Women of a Certain Age.* New York: Harper & Row, Pubs., 1979.

Sarton, May. *At Seventy.* New York: W. W. Norton & Co., 1984.

Scarf, Maggie. *Unfinished Business: Pressure Points in the Lives of Women.* New York: Doubleday & Co., 1980.

Secunda, Victoria. *By Youth Possessed: The Denial of Age in America.* New York: Bobbs-Merrill Co., 1984.

Seskin, Jane. *More Than Mere Survival: Conversations with Women Over 65.* New York: Newsweek, 1980.

Shields, Laurie. *Displaced Homemakers: Organizing for a New Life.* New York: McGraw-Hill Book Co., 1981.

Index

About the Author

Jane Seskin—author of nine books including *Living Single, Getting My Head Straight,* and *A Time to Love* and coauthor of *Older Women/Younger Men*—is a contributor to numerous national magazines and newspapers.

A former elementary school teacher and supervisor of students at NYU, Ms. Seskin has been a facilitator for both single women and co-ed groups. She has taught writing and led publishing workshops and has been on the faculty of Hunter College, Marymount, the YWCA Women's Center, and the New School for Social Research.

She currently lectures throughout the country on social problems and interpersonal relations and is a frequent guest on radio and television.

Photograph by Mary Manilla.

Other AARP Books